Books Speak For You books may be ordered through booksellers or by contacting:
Booksspeakforyou.com
The views expressed in this work are solely those of the Author, Justin Brown.

Any illustration provided by iStock and such images are being used for illustrative purposes.
Certain stock imagery © iStock.
ISBN:978-1-64050-292-5
Library of Congress Control Number: 2017907232
Printed in the United States of America

Praise for
Ugh!?! Not Another Diversity Book!

"Very high energy book, easy ideas to incorporate with very basic ideas presented in a new and exciting way. Recommend starting a "D.A.P." program at other universities."

"Very impressive, a talented, passionate and dedicated student affairs leader with wonderful ideas and sincerity."

"Excellent book! Interactive & well organized and the enthusiasm was contagious."

"The book is all that! Our first year students read it for their orientation readings!"

"Very inspiring, a gifted soul the author has to be to create a piece like this!"

Ugh!?! Not Another Diversity Book!

"When Multicultural Competence Meets A Real Reality."

Written By: Justin LaKyle Brown

Acknowledgement

First and foremost, let me say this…God has blessed me with many gifts and talents, and writing is certainly not one of them. I had to verbally record this book, have it transcribed, and then have it translated into text. Talk about a long process, right? Unfortunately for me, writing is one of my weaknesses but I believe that weaknesses are just excuses, so I continued to press forward.

The problem with acknowledging individuals or even writing an acknowledgement page is that I'm sure that I will omit someone. This isn't done intentionally, however, it is just the fact that there have been so many inspirational and influential people in my life. If you are reading this and you swear that you were supposed to be acknowledged, I apologize in advance for forgetting to mention you. Please charge it to my head and not my heart.

At the outset, to all of the people who challenged me to write this book, well, HERE IT IS. For those of you who are not aware of the journey, this book has been 10 years in the making. It is a combination of not having enough time, lack of self-confidence, and willpower to finish it. I have completed my goal and it's now finally done (Air High-Five)!

I would like to take time to personally thank Emily Bolick for her excellent editorial skills, knowledge, and patience. Emily, thank you for all of your encouragement, updates, and countless hours of helping me. I know I had a lot to say to get this book written.

Thank you to my church family. Some of you were present when I was a child, watched me grow up, and encouraged these talents within me. There certainly is a special place for all of you in my heart. Thank you for being a family I could come to, even when my family was available.

To the professors and student affairs professionals who challenged me, guided me, and encouraged me in my lifetime, you all are the REAL MVP. Please know that I am just one result of the many successes you may have had with students in your teaching career. Continue to teach with purpose and encourage with determination.

To my magnificent students, you are the reason I do this. Thank you for the countless hours of laughter, tears, hugs, and understandings. You have given me an adequate amount of content, stories, and experiences to last a lifetime. You have brought so much joy to my life. Thank you for providing me the excitement I possessed to come into work each and every day!

A special thanks is extended to those who read portions of this book for clarity, content, and understanding. I appreciate you taking time out of your busy lives to assist me. Dina Torrie, Emily Powers, Kimberly Brown, Jocelyn Brown, Laura Brown, and Pamela Brown, you helped me to make this happen.

Foreword (A Letter)

By Justin L. Brown (2073)

Greetings Justin,

If I have done this correctly, this letter should have reached you in 2017, you know, the time period when you are actually writing this book. Suppose for a second that time travel is a real thing! Come on...take a quick second and conceptualize that. Well in the future (2073), it still isn't, so don't get your hopes up. But, we are able to send small objects into the past, just haven't successfully been able to send humans through yet. Nevertheless, how are you? I don't want to mess up the timeline too much by sending this letter to you, but hey, who can say they wrote their own forward, huh? A foreword is a (usually short) piece of writing that is generally written by someone other than the primary author. Typically, there is a connection between the writer of the forward and the book's primary author. What better connection than it actually being the author? I would argue that we are two different people Justin! Granted, we share the same DNA, but who I am today and who you are there in 2017 are completely different people.

Again, I don't want to alter the future, however, I do want to provide you with some insight. Things are a bit better in the future, not perfect, but better. Eventually you have this realization that you cannot resolve everything on your own and that it's on everyone to impel our society forward regarding diversity, inclusion, and multiculturalism. You must agree, things are getting better right? Oh yeah, you're in 2017, just wait until the year 2020. Things got a lot better, I promise.

I recollect the excitement when we initially conceptualized the thought of writing a book. The book began to breathe life the moment the title was created. I remember it going through several versions and rough drafts – but it finally came to fruition. By book 76, Justin, you honestly become tired of writing. Eventually, this book will take on a life of its own.

Originally, your words were intended for an audience to hear, but most importantly, this book served as a true reminder and critical key for why you do what you do now. At this point, it's time for you to figure out how you will present this book to the universe…whoops, did I say that? I meant to say, how would you present this book to THE WORLD?

You've met a lot of interesting people during your lifetime. Some of who will have had an instant recognition by their celebrity names. There are some who may have been simply on the subway during your travels from university to university doing public speaking. You began to ask yourself some significant questions. Whose story means more to you? Who will tell their story for them? Most importantly, how will you convey your message in a short book? Will you get everything out? Will you pull from personal experiences? Do you even want to let people into your life? All are very good and relevant questions. Regardless of what you decide to do, you'll be fine. The future is bright for everyone. For you, your family, your friends, and mostly importantly your readers. Seriously, you didn't think time travel would be a thing? COME ON!

Regardless of what you think, always keep pushing forward. Never take "No." for an answer and always put your trust in GOD. Good luck to you in writing this book, it's going to be a tough undertaking, but eventually it will be well worth it. I look forward to reading the edited version in the future.

Sincerely,

Justin L. Brown, Ph.D.

Dedication

To my family

To my wonderful and determined parents who pushed me and believed in me, even when I didn't believe in myself, I am so grateful. Thank you for your words of wisdom to me as well as the many days and nights of fervent prayers.

To my grandparents who set the stage and foundation while ensuring that their children and grandchildren valued education. All while tirelessly committing to safeguarding that our family stayed together.

To my wonderful siblings, you make life enjoyable. You bring joy and happiness to my life, I love you all.

Dina, Pamela, Kim, Emily, Laura, I appreciate your time and dedication on this piece. Without you, it could not have been possible. Your tireless efforts, energy, and time are sincerely appreciated. This is just as big as an accomplishment for you all as it is for me. I could not have done it without out.

To My Lord and Savior

Without having Jesus Christ in my life, I am nothing. Although, I am never certain what you have in store for my life, I will continue to follow you and always love you. I am thankful for HIS role and presence in my life. Thank you, Father. The Highest praise belongs to you. Thank you again for giving me strength and wisdom and for never letting me go.

Editor's Note
Emily A. Bolick, M.Ed.

I never thought I would one day be an editor. Like the author, I am a student affair professional and my education focused on counseling, student development, communications, gender studies, and sociology. These are subjects I am passionate about because I want to understand people, provide support, challenge their thinking, and help them become agents of change. I became an editor when I saw the opportunity to be part of something great. I happen to be friends and colleagues with a man who is trying to make a difference and change this world. I wanted to do my part to ensure that his voice, knowledge, and experiences got out there. That people, regardless of where you are geographically, had the opportunity to hear, or I guess read, what he has to say. That you can take this book and use what you have learned to do something to make this world a better place. That you will be encouraged to be the best possible version of yourself that you can be.

I wanted to take a moment to address some of the topics in this book. Justin is going to cover some intense issues – issues that may be difficult to understand and may trigger emotional or psychological responses. Throughout this book, there will be discussions of racism, hate crimes, white privilege and guilt, power-based violence, unjustified death, sexual assault, rape, and the mistreatment of minority groups. I want you to know that you are not alone. If something brings up negative thoughts or reminds you of past experiences, there are people who want to help you. Below are some national resources if you ever need them, but youcan certainly find one in your local community. Never be afraid to ask for help.

National Sexual Assault Telephone Hotline

1-800-656-HOPE (4673)

National Child Abuse Hotline

1-800-4-A-Child

National Resource Center on Domestic Violence

1-800-537-2238

National Center for Victims of Crime

202-467-8700

National Disability Rights Network

202-408-9514

GLBT National Hotline

1-888-843-4564

National Suicide Prevention Lifeline

call 1-800-273-8255 *or text* 741-741

National Violence Against Women Prevention Research Center

(843) 792-2945

Contents

Chapter 1
The Beginning

Welcome! So, you think that you were big and bad enough to pick up this book. Well, maybe it was because you saw the cover. Maybe it was because you have to read it for class, or maybe you just thought this title was too interesting to pass up. Regardless of the reason, I'm glad you picked it up because there's going to be some interesting topics that we will be talking about. Speaking of interesting, I should've known that I was going to have an interesting life. It wasn't from the fact that I had an opportunity to write a book, or from the fact that I received my master's degree. It wasn't even for the reason that I have met over 300 celebrities or because I have been to four different continents. It's definitely not because I have over 300 followers on Instagram (which is not that many) but seriously, maybe we should really look at how my life started.

You know it's the same old story, high school basketball star meets beautiful woman and the two fall in love. Then they become high school sweethearts, and boom here comes me. But actually, this story is very different because I decided that I wanted to be born on a highway! Yes, a highway! On the day of my birth, my parents were driving and my mom started having contractions. There wasn't enough time for her to get to the hospital. I decided I wanted to meet the world and there was nothing she could do about it. My mom and I were flown to the hospital in a helicopter and made it just in time. Get it? JUST-IN time? Corny, huh?

I want you, the reader, to know that I am just a normal guy. I love take-out just like you. I love Netflix (no chill)...let's just try Netflix and snacks. I love to sleep in and like you, I probably wish that Chick-fil-A were open on Sundays. I know there are people out there who wish Five-Below sold clothes, and like many of you, I love spending money on stuff that I don't need. I enjoy silly cat videos on YouTube, playing old Super

Nintendo games, and eating Dunkaroos. I continue to watch *Fresh Prince* reruns and I think that *Batman, The Animated Series*, was the best cartoon of all time. But is there more to me? Well, my middle name is LaKyle. When I walked across the stage to get my master's degree they pronounced it Justin LACKEEL Brown. When I got back to my seat, my friend looked at me and said, "LAKEEL? What's that?" I said "It's Hebrew, shhh!" You see, every Black mother wants to give her child an interesting name. Most people call it "ghetto," but some Black folk call it unique. Some parents go as far as to even name their children Uniqua. My mother said she didn't want that for me, so instead, she gave me a "ghetto" middle name. She said that if anybody ever asked what the "L" stood for when I became famous, just say that it stood for Lawrence.

What I find most interesting about all of this is that my mom owned and operated a child daycare center when I was growing up. The center was called Kim's Kreative Kids. As my youngest sister, who has a dark sense of humor, so cleverly points out, the acronym equals K.K.K. I think that was my first introduction to diversity. My mom had a very diverse day care of kids. There were about 15-20 kids from all different races. If you came to my parent's house, you would think that she had a small group of Planeteers from around the world. You might think that you were looking at the cast of *The Magic School Bus* or maybe you just thought that you stepped into *It's a Small World After All*. I really do think that was my first introduction to diversity because we had kids who were white, Asian, Black, Hispanic, and kids with disabilities. I never thought anything was wrong with this picture, it is just how life was. So when I would go and play with the kids, I didn't see any issues with color, ability, or ethnicity. Again, I was five. This time period of my life was right around when *Power Rangers* was a popular TV show. I know that every single time we played *Power Rangers*, they made me the Black Ranger. I didn't know why, but it happened. But even as kids, we just wanted to go and have some fun. There were no social constructs or rules. By the age of 3, 4, or even 5, you're not yet fully programmed to think a certain way. I didn't know

14

that I was a Black kid or that one of my best friend was white and that the other was Hispanic.

I don't think I realized I was Black until the sixth grade. I remember going to the mall; we have a few malls in the area where I grew up. We had the Exton Square Mall, which is just an average, local mall. Then we had the King of Prussia Mall, which is the second largest mall in the US. This story takes place at the Exton Square Mall. When I was in the sixth grade, probably about 10 years old, I remember stepping into a store called Suncoast. Special shout out to all those people who remember Suncoast – there were many stores like it such as Sam Goody or F Y E. Anyway, I remember it was wintertime and my mom always made me wear a heavy coat. It was pretty big and it wasn't fashionable. It wasn't made to be fashionable, it was made to keep me warm. Of course my mom was the only mom making me wear one and made sure that it was buttoned all the way up before I left. I can hear her now, "You got money to go to the doctor? No? Then I suggest you put on that coat then!" Unfortunately, it was her rules. It was either follow her rules and get a ride to the mall, or you can stay at home and be on AIM messenger. For those who remember AIM messenger, take a moment to know that you are very old.

Anyway, as soon as I got to the mall, first thing I would do was take off the coat. I would ball it up and put it under my arm. You know, I was trying to be cool with my friends. I didn't want to wrap it around my waist or wear it like a cape because that wasn't cool. I remember going into Suncoast and checking out all of the VHS tapes. As I was walking around, it felt like someone was following me. I wasn't really paying too much attention to it at the time. But when I was about to leave the store, I remember two people being at the front. They looked directly at me and said, "Sir where are you going?" I said, "I'm leaving." and they said, "We need you to come here with us." I went to where they told me to go and the manager demanded that I shake out my coat. At the time, I didn't know I was being racially profiled. I actually didn't know why he asked me to do that. So I shook out my coat and he said, "Oh I'm sorry." But in

15

my mind, I was like, shake out my coat for what? The manager didn't say anything else; he just walked away and I left. I remember coming home and telling my mom that story and how furious and angry she was. That was the first time I actually realized that racial tensions and racial barriers were a real thing and that I had been racially profiled. That was the first time that I came to realize that I was Black.

I come from Coatesville, PA. For all of you who don't know where that is, we're famous for two things. We're famous for basketball star Rip "Rip City" Hamilton and the steel that was manufactured at Lukens Steel Company. Some of the steel was actually used for the Twin Towers at the World Trade Center. But most importantly, we're a big sports town. A lot of people comment, "Oh, Coatesville – you guys destroyed us in basketball." or "You destroyed us in football." Then, other people don't know us at all, so they say, Coatesville, you make coats there; it's actually not a funny joke. In Coatesville, everybody co-exists. I mean white people, Hispanic people, Black people, Asian people, LGBTQIA people – they all live together. It's almost a reflection of how my mom's daycare was when I was growing up. So again, I didn't think anything was different. I didn't think I was being introduced to diversity because this is what I remember. It's a small city, at the bottom part of Southeast Pennsylvania about maybe fifty minutes outside Philadelphia. You see people from all different walks of life, people from diverse backgrounds, religions, ethnicities, sexual orientation, origins, and cultural backgrounds. None of these differences seemed like a big deal to me.

I never thought that writing a book was going to be something that I would ever do. I had a high school teacher, (who would probably kill me if he knew that I was telling this story) Mr. Morton, who always told us that we should be better than what we think we are. Whenever I would turn in my essays in class, I always told him, "Hey, I'm not a good writer." He would reply, "You're as good as you think you are." I've followed up with him later on in my life but I'll always remember the things that he left us with in high school. One of

16

the biggest stories that Mr. Morton taught us was the day that he knew he was going to marry his wife. What happened was, his wife had been out of town for a little bit and her sister called him because she needed help with her plumbing. He asked her, "Why don't you ask your dad?" She said, "Because I know you will come over and help." Mr. Morton said he remembered going over to his now sister-in-law's place and she was sitting in her panties at the top of the stairs. She said, "I really need my pipes fixed; let's see if you can fix them." Mr. Morton said he ran out of that room as fast as he could. He said when he got outside of the apartment, everyone from his girlfriend's family was there. They were all sitting there clapping and were so happy. He said he remembers exactly how his wife felt. She came up to him and said, "I love you." She was crying and everyone said, "Welcome to the family." That's when he knew he was going to marry her. On the last day of school, he asked the class what they thought the moral of the story was. I remember being the first person to raise my hand, as always, and I said, "The moral of the story is to always do right by your girlfriend." and he said, "No." Everybody else then started giving their answers and thoughts. Someone said, "The moral of the story is to always do the right thing." He said, "No." Someone else said, "The moral of the story is be a man of your word." He still said "No." As we were all walking out of the class, he said, "The moral of the story is, never leave your condoms in your car. Have a great summer everyone!" We all left the class puzzled. I was the last one out of the room and Mr. Morton pulled me aside and said, "I want to let you know, that story didn't happen." I couldn't believe it! So he explained, "I just wanted to give you a funny plot twist because that's very much how life is. Life is like a funny plot twist." I remember telling Mr. Morton, "Thank you so much for everything you did for me this year, you were a great teacher." He reminded me, "Continue to be better than you are." He encouraged me to keep writing. Well, like Mr. Morton said, life is pretty much like a plot twist.

During my senior year, I was trying hard to find the perfect college for me;there are so many colleges out there. I had been accepted to about 30 different schools, none of which were giving me the money I really needed. And all those "promises" of scholarships for African-American men didn't seem like it was going to happen. One day, I stumbled upon this little school about an hour north of Pittsburgh called Slippery Rock University. Yes, you heard me right, Slippery Rock University. It's actually a real place, you should look it up. There are a lot of legends about Slippery Rock and how it got its name, but the one that they refer to the most is this: During the colonial times, there were soldiers who were being chased by the local Seneca Nation of Indians. At the time, the troops were wearing very large and heavy boots. They were able to cross the rivers and the creeks in the forest area where they were being chased. But, the Seneca warriors weren't wearing boots; they were wearing moccasins. The Seneca slipped on the rocks – Slippery Rock. There's actually a famous battle that's reenacted every year. George Washington stayed in a cabin outside Slippery Rock – it's this whole big thing. At this point in my world, all I was exposed to was a very diverse community. And, being a PK (for those who don't know, that stands for a Preacher's kid), I was taught to treat everybody as you would want them to treat you. Everyone in my church was multicultural. Everyone in my community was multicultural. Everyone in the daycare and everyone in all the schools that I attended growing up were multicultural. I really didn't think that anything outside of this existed. But then I got to Slippery Rock and found out that I was the only pepper in the milk! At the time, in 2007, Slippery Rock's diversity enrollment rate was at 6%. That means I rarely saw anyone who looked like me, not my professors, not my colleagues, not the student leaders, not anyone. It was pretty much just me. It taught me some really valuable lessons. It taught me that you're going to have to step out of your comfort zone to be a leader. You might not have all the leadership skills right now, but you're going to develop them. I learned a lot about my cultural identity during my four years there.

I wanted to be a Psychology major. I found out a little bit about Freud during Psychand I said, "SIKE!" I ended up finding out that Communications is where I wanted to be, not knowing yet that Communications was going to take me somewhere great. I had two classes that really stuck out to me at Slippery Rock – Human Diversity and Intercultural Communications. I think it was through these two classes that I found a love for diversity. It wasn't just something I lived; it was something I wanted to strive for. After taking those classes, I decided that I needed to do something at Slippery Rock that was going to leave a legacy. I wanted something that was going to be worthwhile, so I created a diversity program from the ground up.

Essentially, the program was designed to bring all the students together on campus for active and engaging conversations along with facilitated games and activities. I wanted to start a student group. I wanted it to be great. I wanted everybody to see me as more than just a Black man. I wanted them to see a strong individual who had a lot of drive and leadership. Since there was little diversity on campus, some of the conversations I was having with people revolved around me being the first person of color (or colored person) they ever talked to. They wanted to know since I was from the Philadelphia area, did I have a gun? People asked if they could touch my hair and I said, "Nah, we have a problem here." These awkward interactions were the genesis of this program. We started off very small in a closet, but we grew and broke the fire code. We moved to the multi-purpose room, but we grew and broke the fire code. Then we moved to the biggest space on campus, the Alumni House, where we met every Tuesday at 7:00pm. Our average weekly attendance was ninety students. That is ninety students who were attending a program outside their curriculum to talk about diversity, cultural awareness, and multiculturalism. There's something special about a student, who has little to no training regarding diversity, who is able to enact such a change. More importantly, the changes were happening outside of the program. I started seeing things change in the dining halls, in the classrooms, and in the residence halls. People were becoming integrated due to the lessons they were learning in this program.

Then came the day when someone contacted me and asked if I was the student who was organizing the diversity programs at Slippery Rock University. I said, "I sure am." They said, "We love that program. We want you to bring it to our institution." So I did! Then I got a call from another school and another school and another school. That's when I knew there was something about this diversity thing, something about supporting communities that embrace and celebrate differences. There was something about having a dialogue about diversity and striving for excellence, respect, and friendship that was driving this program. Little did I know, in my junior year I would travel to 15 different schools to develop different programs on college campuses. This was as a student; I didn't even have my bachelor's degree yet. What kind of expert was I? I certainly didn't see myself as an expert at the time. Sure, I had gotten a full ride to Slippery Rock University and was very active on campus. I later received a full ride to Indiana University of Pennsylvania for graduate school. Well, my next step in life, getting into one of the top ten master's programs in the country helped me with this self-actualization. But at age 20, was I really an expert?

I entered a field called Student Affairs in Higher Education. The student affairs field is composed of all of the offices, departments, and services available to students outside of the academic realm at a college or university. I feel like a lot of the learning that happens with students happens outside of the classroom. If you go to school for just the classroom experience, you're missing out on a part of your college career. I learned a lot about myself through that master's program; it challenged me academically, it pushed me intellectually, and made me reach as far as I could. I learned a lot about diversity and I ended up coming out of the program with a fully developed company. So when I left Slippery Rock, I was able to leave the program behind and I ended up writing my first training manual called Diversity Awareness Program. This is what actually turned into what the company is known as today; The Diversity Awareness Program (D.A.P.). It was really special because at the time, my first year as a grad student, I had traveled to about 45 different schools just talking about diversity and bringing people together in unity to challenge stereotypes and change perceptions. Then the time came for me to really take this thing on the road. I paid extreme attention to what I wanted to do with this program and it really blossomed. It makes me think back to the quote "We hold these truths to be self-evident that all men are created equal." As I was growing up and started un-programming myself, I became aware that NOT ALL men are created equal. Even more, I thought, why did it have to be all men, why couldn't it be all women as well? What if you don't identify as a man or woman, what if you're gender non-binary or genderqueer? None of these things made sense to me until I really started getting on the road with this program and hearing from my audiences.

The program is very simple. D.A.P.'s mission is to promote diversity and cultural awareness in all aspects of life to students, faculty, and staff on a university campus. This is done through active and engaging discussions on social trends, issues, and ideas. D.A.P. serves as a resourceful tool and encourages students and community members to seek opportunities to become more culturally aware and conscious. D.A.P. has educated staff, students, faculty, officers of the law, and Fortune 500 companies by inviting a diverse group of people together to participate in activities that not only help them in small groups, but also take those discussion topics out to the global community. Some could say, "Justin, are you telling me that this program holds twohour sessions, and you're playing games, participating in activities, and building ice breakers?" That's exactly what I'm telling you! Why? In a two hour period, I can take a group of 80 strangers and make them closer than any friends they have ever known. Why? I've discovered that individuals like to be heard. Individuals like to have fun. Individuals like competition and individuals really like to open up. You are probably sitting there saying, "I'm an individual and I don't like to open up." Seriously, think to yourself – sometimes don't you just want to be heard? Don't you want somebody to just feel you and understand what you're saying? Don't you want

21

to say something one time and know that people get you and get your thoughts? Everybody wants to be cared about and everybody wants to know that they are special. That's what this program does.

I was able to expand upon this program when I became a Resident Director.I live and work on a campus. I oversee a building of 700 students. It is very fascinating job and life! It is like being in a nature documentary. You get to observe students' living habits, their eating habits, their bathing habits, and their mating habits. I even get to see some of their tribal rituals – meaning when their herd moves. Essentially, that's on a Thirsty Thursday when I see a group of 60 students all leaving the building at one time, at 11:00pm...with their backpacks on. I guess they are going to the library. You get to see their migration patterns. Being a Resident Director and living amongst the students has been one of the most beneficial things that has ever happened to me. You get to see your student's development from the first day that they move in until they leave. The students that leave are so much different from when they first started. Needless to say, they gave me a lot of material for this program.

We're going to dive into this program throughout the book. I think it's really important to know that I am not an expert but I am persistently trying to fine-tune and improve my craft. I may have been doing this for the past 10 years but I promise you, I started out where some of you are now – learning about diversity, culture awareness, and multiculturalism. I say this because I don't think that anyone can be a total expert; no one knows it all! However, while you are reading this book, I want you to keep in mind that this is from the vantage point of someone who has visited over 400 schools, presented, and seen this program in nine different modules over 600 times. I have also read countless books about diversity, multiculturalism, social justice, microaggression, and cultural awareness. I want you to know that I'm speaking from the heart of someone who has learned, someone who has read, someone who has been taught, and someone who has experienced. I want to apologize in advance. Some things you learn about the differences of other people – the way that they think, live, and carry themselves – you will not be able to learn in a book. If you're somebody who has picked up this book for entertainment, you're in luck. If you're someone who has picked up this book so that you could learn something, you're in luck. If you're someone who picked up this book because you wanted to become more aware of your own differences, you're in luck. If you're someone who picked up this book because you're really trying to jump into the heart and mind of Justin LaKyle Brown, well, you're in luck as well. None of us are experts in diversity. This material is based off of the experiences that I have had, things that I have seen, and literature that I've read. So student affairs professionals, you won't find theories here or any of the theorist who guides our practices, this is not what this book is about. This book is about the adventures and life lessons learned by Justin LaKyle Brown. So, sit back, enjoy, and let's go on this journey together.

Chapter 2
This or That

Congratulations, you made it this far. I'm guessing that if Chapter 1 didn't scare you off and you want to continue reading, hopefully you'll read to the end of this chapter. That's my goal. Considering that I've never written a book before, I am quite excited and thrilled to share my experiences with you. So please forgive my enthusiasm if I seem to be all over the place. I think that this same sentiment reflects my life. Life is kind of like a game of this or that. I'll say this over and over; I've done this program at about 400 different schools. I've done these modules and activities on diversity more than 600 times. I find it interesting when I'm traveling and people ask, "Justin, how do you come up with these activities? Some of these things are really controversial. How do you get an idea and just go with it?" The short answer is that sometimes ideas just come to me. I've driven around western PA for a long time while going to school. When I'm driving on the turnpike, I get bored, so I may come up with a particular game. For example, let me count how many Confederate flags I see on my way to my next event. On this particular day, I counted sixteen. I try to come up with games that are going to be thought provoking. I try to come up with games and activities that are going to get individuals speaking. Here's my thing, when I'm presenting these programs, I don't want individuals to have an activity where they can possibly provide the close-ended answers of yes or no. This is because the programs are never about me, they're always about the participants. I need to hear their soul and hear their mind. I need to hear their experiences. I need to hear about what they've been programmed to think. These are the things I need to unravel.

The goal of most of my programs is to get participants to learn and unlearn – to deprogram themselves so they can start looking and thinking through a wider lens. Throughout the book, I'm going to talk about a lot of different themes and experiences. This brings us to one of the most popular games we conduct is called *This or That*. Essentially, I give two topics to choose from and the participants have to go to this side or that side. Like most of my games, I like to throw in a monkey wrench. The monkey wrench in this game is, there is no middle; you must pick a side. You would think these instructions were simple, right? No, people start to get uncomfortable when you take their ability to have the middle ground. Most people like to stay neutral when it comes to decisions. No one likes to offend, no one likes to muddy the water, and no one wants people to judge them. My ability to take away their neutral zone, their Switzerland you might say, really invokes some feelings. I tell everybody, we're going to start off with very easy topics then the topics will get a little harder.

Let me take you through some examples of this activity and introduce you to the participant's reactions. The first topic is *Cats or Dogs*. Some people go to the cat side, others go to the dog side. In almost every program I've done, there are at least ten times more people on the dog side than on the cat side. I always go to the lesser side first. So in this instance, I go to the cat side to talk to the people. These cat people really love cats! I didn't know until I started doing this program that some people actually like animals more than they like people. For my cat lovers out there, you really love your cats. So, I talk to some of these people on the cat side and I hear things like, "I love my cats." and "My cats are so great." I say to them, "Wait, timeout! Cats with an S?" I hear the reply of, "Yes, I have five cats." At this point, I give them the side-eye; no judgment thrown to anyone out there with five cats! They talk about cats being cuddly and how they love them. They talk about how the cats always look out for them and they don't hurt them like some people do. The dog people on the other side are saying, "Dogs are great!" and "Dogs are always happy to see you." They say, "Dogs are loyal." Then the cat people start talking again, "Cats are independent. They don't need you." Then the dog people counter, "You can train dogs to do what you want or need" or "Have you ever seen a seeing-eye cat?" This is where the spark happens. The spark ignites in a moment's time, and with it I am able to pull myself out of the situation. My goal as the facilitator is to get the sparks to fly, to get people having conversations without me – 80% them, 20% me. Then things continue to get just a little bit more interesting.

We talk about *Textingor Calling*. Individuals who seem to have closer relationships like calling so they can hear the other person's voice and inflection. While the people who like to text are usually more direct and to the point. Their thought is, look, I just need to tell you what's on my mind or get this information out there. Texting gives me time to figure out what I need and how to say it. If we text, I have the ability to not text you back if I want, or to reflect more before I reply. It really starts to make people think. During the session, people are allowed to change sides at any time. If they hear some of the comments from others and like what they hear, they can change sides. The two topics we just talked about aren't controversial. It isn't until we get to the deeper subjects that people really start coming out of their comfort zone.

For example, we do a subject called *Love or Money*. Now this one is really interesting because the majority of people go over to the love side but there are always a few people who stay on the money side. I step over to speak with the people who chose money. I say to them, "Oh, my gosh! Why did you choose money?Is it because you like to make it rain?" They reply, "No, I don't have money like that." So I say, "Oh, then you must grab a whole fist full of pennies to make it hail." This is usually a pretty great joke to get some crowd laughter. Then the people on the money side start speaking and you can see that they have a lot of things in common. The people who really want the money say they work hard for what they have, money can provide them with the happiness that they need, and some say, money will never run out on you. We always take the opportunity to really dive deep into what people say. People talk about the people they love, significant others wholeft, people who've had divorces and lost their money, or they saw issues within their families. These are big components in diversity. People's viewpoints are based off of their own personal experiences, not things that they'd

26

necessarily been taught or programmed to think. The things you see on TV, things you see in the media, and things you learned in school are all abstracts that program people. But, the other half of what people do is learned from their experiences. They learn through what they've personally been through and what they have observed around them.

After talking to the money people, I step over and talk to the people on the love side. They're all just so in love, but most aren't even talking about their own love. What they're trying to do is get the people over on the money side to think about how they feel. I find this so fascinating because the game is called *This or That* meaning you have the ability to think for yourself. When it comes to love or money, the people who are on the love side are always trying to convince the money people otherwise. They say, "Money is not going to keep you warm." and "When you're old and all you have is money, it won't *be* there for you." They add, "Money won't be there for you when you're sick." Instead of talking about why they chose love, all they see are the people on the other side who didn't choose love and that becomes what's most important to them. It shows me that individuals sometimes have one-track minds. They really want people to see things how they see it – not necessarily trying to understand that everybody has differences and sees things differently. That's why I think the game *This or That* is so important. We really get to unearth people's opinions, their stances, and their experiences because when you're going from one side to the other side, you don't have the ability to hide. You have to be able to back up your concepts by standing on one side or the other.

Another controversial topic is *Church or No Church*. As soon as I call this one out, everyone is hesitant to move and choose their side. Most people wait to see what other people are going to do and then they start moving accordingly. Growing up as a Pastor's kid, I saw church very differently than how other people saw it. My dad always taught me that you welcome everybody who comes into the church – everyone from all walks of life are always welcome in God's house. It didn't matter what the person's situation was, you welcomed everybody. To say that these people are wrong or not worthy goes against the mission of the church. We all have things to work on. To see people in the church and tell them they need to fix something is wrong if you don't point the finger right back at yourself and ask, "What do I need to fix?" It wasn't until I got out of my hometown that I realized that there are people that really hate churches and have had really negative experiences. Throughout these games, I saw that there were more people on the *No Church* side than on the *Church* side. I always let the lesser side, in this case the *Church* side, go first. They say, "It's a place where I can find myself." and "It's a place where I can feel at home." Someone usually adds, "It's a place where I can get my spiritual rejuvenation to get me through the week." The people on the other side don't feel that way. The people on the other side are usually there because they've had a bad experience at church or in the religious community. They say, "I used to go to church but those people don't practice what they preach." or "They're only out for money." Some even say "It's a place built on lies." I started to notice that people were having really bad experiences in churches and this touched me deeply. This was never my experience in my church, but it seems that has been the experience for many people out there.

While we have people who have good experiences and bad, we also have someone in the group who points out, "What about those individuals who don't go to 'church'?" I always do my best to ignore these people because they will be integral to the discussion at the end. This game is either this or that; there is no middle. I made them choose church even though there may be people who attend other houses of worship in the audience. In this case, they may not worship in church, but maybe are Jewish and worship in synagogue or may be Muslim and worship in a mosque. Or for those people who don't go to church when they're at home because they worship at St. Mattress or Bedside Baptist. It isn't until we get to the next two topics, that things get more thought provoking

One of them is the topic of *Privilege or No Privilege.*

How people see themselves in this world is really important here because it developed their perspective. The college students are often talking about each other when they participate in this one since they are physically moving; there seems to be a lot more judgment occurring. The people who choose the *Privilege* side say, "Well I rather have privilege than not have it." They say that people who don't have privilege go through life in a harder way. I hear them say "I'm in college, so I should be on the privilege side because I'm privileged to get an education." I always ask, "Why do you think those people are over there?" but no one usually can give an answer. Then I ask the people on the *No Privilege* side how they feel. They say, "Until everyone can have privilege, no one can have it." and "I recognize that I was privileged growing up and I realized that some of my privileges may have taken away the privileges of others." These people are self-aware of their own privileges and they're willing to forego their privileges to ensure that everyone can be on an equal playing field. It's really fascinating when people start sharing and it shows perspective. This is something I am trying to help them understand; that your views and understandings vary because of your experiences.

Privilege can be hard to understand. It is when you think something is not a problem because it's not a problem for you personally. Everyone goes through difficult situations in life, but the experience can be vastly different depending on your level of privilege. What you start to realize is when people are switching sides, they're not doing it because of their race, gender, sexual orientation, and so on. They're switching sides based on their beliefs. This really breaks down stereotypes and the misconceptions like "All Black people do this." or "All white people do that." In this activity, the participants can see the thoughts and reasoning as to why someone chose their side. They see that it is not based on the color of their skin or where they were born. Sure, these can be part of the process, a factor in their perspective, but it isn't the end all be all. There is so much more that goes into how a person views the world than just one aspect of their identity.

The last topic is really important, *Gay or No Gay*. The participants are really confused about this one. They want to know what "no gay" means, but that's the point, they have to interpret it themselves – we want to discuss how they saw the options. The results are generally split with a good amount of people on both sides. When I ask the *No Gay* side, they say, "Because I'm not gay." or "I chose no gay because I don't personally identify with being a homosexual." When I go over to the *Gay* side, I hear, "I chose this because I do support gay rights." or "I'm an ally." We talk about how being an ally is more than just saying something; you have to be involved. You have to be dedicated and supportive to the movement, you have to do something! Being an ally is about action, it's not just a status. As you can see, there are all these little educational moments inside the larger purpose. They are just as important and need to be covered. After we have some discussion, we hear some more reasoning. Some chose the *Gay* side because they are gay. Others defend the *No Gay* saying, "I'm not over here because I'm a hater or against gay people." or "I'm not someone who doesn't believe in LGBTQIA rights, I just don't identify."

It's really interesting what people think about each other based on where they stand. If you take a look at all of these concepts, you don't know why people stood on a particular side, but a lot of people jump to conclusions and make assumptions about that person. When the activity is over, we process it all. Generally, they say it was fun, but really hard. When I ask them why they feel this way I hear, "Well the game forced us to go left or right; this or that." I say to the team, "Well, that's crazy because in American life, it seems like we only have two races that always fight. Which races do you think are those that are always fighting?" The group responds, "Black and white. Oh, I get it, that's how this game is...this or that, black or white." There has to be some gray area in there and the gray consists of all the diversity and all the different backgrounds, cultures, races, religions, sexual orientations, and abilities that the world has to offer. Things cannot be black or white – there has to be a gray area.

30

Some people say, "I don't like how you forced us to go on one side or the other; there was no middle. It didn't give me the ability to choose." I reply, "How many of you felt like you were forced to believe something from your parents when you were growing up?" You would be surprised at all the hands that go up. Then, we start talking about that. People say, "Well, my parents taught me not to trust people of color." or "My parents taught me that being gay is wrong." I often hear "My parents taught me that religion was the only way." and "My parents weren't parents at all and didn't teach me anything." These things have really shaped the framework and mindsets of these students. I ask, "How many of you have been taught things by a religious organization, and now that you're a little bit older, and have gone through some things, realize that it isn't necessarily true?" Again, you see all the hands go up and you see the wheels churning in their mind. Then I asked them, "How many of you have a friend that swears they know every single thing about everything? That you have to believe what they believe because they're your friend?" The hands go up. To lighten the mood some, I try to throw some jokes in like asking "How many of you don't have a friend like that?" and a few put their hands up. I end it with "Well that means it's you!" I usually get a great laugh with that one and people get more at ease.

The biggest thing we talk about next is that there has to be the possibility of both – you can't just say things are this or that or black or white. There has to be a neutral place where you can go on both sides. Going on both sides doesn't necessarily have to do with your color. Going on both sides could be due to your experience, what you were taught, and how you view the world. Sometimes, picking a side is difficult because each has valuable points depending on how you view it. This can make people nervous or afraid to be judged because people don't know your "why," they just see you picking a side. That's why when we do *Church or No Church* I try to ignore the "Not everyone goes to church." people at the time. We don't always have them, but when we do I try and save it for the end. I think this one emphasizes the gray area the most. It's not *Religious or Not*

Religious or Spiritual Not Spiritual– it's a very specific place of worship. There were participants who are Jewish and attend a synagogue or Muslim and worship in a mosque. But, they still chose church because they didn't want to be judge as not being religious. Even though it wasn't their place of worship, they chose it. No one spoke up that some people go to synagogue or mosque. Why didn't anyone bring this up? People were afraid of being judged, so they went to the *Church*side. The people that chose *No Church*, felt like everyone was judging them. Or, they were judging on the *Love or Money* or they or they were judging them on *Privilege or No Privilege.*

As we are wrapping up *This or That*, I ask "If you're prejudiced, please stand." There are usually about two people who stand. Then I say, "So I guess the rest of you have never judged anybody before you met them? Never came to a conclusion about somebody or had preconceived notions?" Then the entire room stands up! I ask why they didn't get up before and I hear "Justin, I didn't stand up because I was afraid that people were going to judge me." I emphasize that we have to be able to own our own stuff – everyone is prejudiced. I can recall a time when I wanted to get my haircut and my barber wasn't available, so I walked into Supercuts. There were two white ladies working. They were both really friendly and ready to help me. And what did I do? I ran out of there as fast as I could! I'm a diversity facilitator and I judged these two because I thought there was no way they can cut a Black man's hair. We all have things to work on. We are all works in progress. None of us are perfect. So for us to say there's no such thing as prejudice, that's a lie. We're all just a little prejudice because we are scared of the unknown. Some are scared to have experiences with people who don't look like them because they are afraid of what their families or friends might think. It's the uncertainty that makes them have fear about a different situation. I find it interesting because a lot of these abstracts are taught from parents to their children. Parents are afraid, so they then reinforce their wrong ideas and teach them to their children. We need to figure out when this cycle will end. Start thinking about it. What did your parents teach you? What are some concepts you learned from your parents or a religious organization that you later found out were wrong? Now that you're a little older, how differently do you see it? The cycle has to end somewhere.

We have to learn how to deprogram ourselves – learn to unlearn. We begin to be programmed as soon as we're born. Little boys' rooms should be blue, they'll play with planes and trucks and they'll be a businessman. Girls should have a pink room, play with dolls, and be a stay-at-home mom. We have got to break out of these boxes we construct for ourselves. We have to let people be people. Just look at what's happening now in 2017. Recently, our president issued an executive order basically sayingyou can be singled out due to how you pray. That's immoral and unconstitutional. Again, it's a *This or That* situation, and depending on what you choose, it could put you on a different side. We have to be able to talk about those things. The game brings up a lot of different concepts. Where would you fall on any of these topics discussed? Which side would you end up on? How would you base your decisions? Would you base it on how you were raised? Would you base it on how you were taught or what you experienced?

Chapter 3
Stereotypes Phenomenon

Stereotypes shape our expectations about groups who are not like us. But the question is, do you believe stereotypes are accurate? If so, think of the stereotypes you feel are true. When I ask participants this question, I get the same answers: Asians are smart, blondes are ditzy, Black people like chicken, and white people are racists. I then ask where these stereotypes come from. The most frequent response is the media, specifically the news. Did you know "news" stands for notable events, weather, and sports?The news conveys prejudice when it reports "facts" because these facts are wrapped in stories, and the stories are inevitably biased. Thus, if you don't watch the news you're uninformed, and if you do watch the news, you're misinformed. When I asked the group, "What does the media suggest when there is a mass shooting done by someone from the Middle East?" Everyone yells, "TERRORIST!" When I ask them, "What does the media imply when there is a shooting by a Black person?" The answer is usually that they are a thug or gangster. When I ask, "What does the media say when there is a mass shooting and you're white?" Everyone agrees, the media depicts them as mentally ill or having a bad day. These "facts" that so many hold to be true, were weaved from a biased story that is the creation of expectations and stereotypes.

The next activity we do as a group, *Stereotype Charades,* is a natural progression from this point. Everyone in the audience receives a card that that contains a particular class, race, religion, sexual orientation, ethnicity, and so on. To name a few, these include Black male, Native American, white female, person with a disability, feminist, or person from the LGBTQIA community. The goal of this activity is to create an engaging conversation about stereotypes. The instructions are for the participants act out the words on the card while the audiences guess the identity. The outcome here is for the actor to unpack why they portrayed the card the way they did and also why the others guessed those identities. Through this process, the group can see how their experiences dictate not only why they portrayed the identity a particular way, but also why they guessed certain ways.

Let's take a look at some examples of this activity. When the *Nerd* actor steps up, they usually pull their pants up to their neck and talk about all their fun homework. Everyone quickly guesses geek, nerd, Asian, or specifically, Chinese. This opens up the discussion as why they selected Asian or Chinese. People responded with "Well you know, all Asians are smart!" but others counter "Trust me. I'm Chinese, and I'm not smart." Or they say, "I'm Asian, and my brother is an idiot." The group gets a laugh out of it, but it brings in an important point. This guides us into the deeper conversation about our perceptions of others and the stereotypes with which we base them. We look at why Chinese was the only Asian culture identified when it is just one of many. As we are wrapping this card up, I usually ask, "So we all came to the conclusion that not all nerds are Asian, right?" The audience agrees. But what they don't know is that I usually include two *Nerd* cards in the game. We'll get back to that later.

It's funny when someone gets the *Black Male* card. They immediately get a sour look on their face and look at me thinking I'm going to get offended. When you do diversity trainings or work with students, you're going to be talking about culture and background. You must have a solid and firm heart and know that people are trying and they are learning. You can't be easily offended. People are in a learning state and they are very vulnerable. Your next statement or action could shape their entire understanding of people who look like you and their experience in diversity learning. For some people, they don't have to experience being a representation of their entire race or culture. They don't have to be "on" all the time or change who they are depending on what company they are around. This is privilege. Diversity facilitators must want to grow and develop people. Otherwise, you're going to get hurt because sometimes people say things that are highly offensive. As the facilitator, it is your job to not take sides, you must remain objective. It's your job to provide the best possible learning experience. Anyway, back to the *Black Male* card, the person will usually ask a friend to come up, which they're allowed to do in *Stereotype Charades.* They usually give them a highly stylized and complex handshake. This, of course, saves the person who drew the *Black Male* card from acting out something more offensive and awkward than a handshake.

The *Black Female* card is interesting too because depending on your geographic background, people act it out differently. Normally when someone gets the *Black Female* card, they say things such as, "Hey girl, I'm about to fight, let me take my earrings off!" Or they pretend they have a bigger butt. At one particular event at the University of Florida, a Japanese woman acted out the *Black Female* card by saying, "At one point, I was a queen and now I have been lowered to just a sexual object." No one knew what she was referring too. She also said, "I'm the strongest person in my household." No one guessed correctly. Her acting was based upon her experience. She was a foreign exchange student and had been living with a Black family and that was her experience; that was her only perception of a Black female. In the media, do we depict Black women as simply sexual objects or women who just have big butts and big lips? Do they go beyond their hips or is it more than just the Black genes that make the blue jeans tight? More extremely, are Black women even respected in their own culture?

Next comes the *Arab Male* card. Now remember, just because I'm a diversity facilitator, doesn't mean I'm not human; I've mademistakes and assumptions. The *Arab Male* card gives me an opportunity to tell this story. I remember being on a plane with my family traveling to Orlando for vacation. This occurred right after the 9/11 and people were on high alert for anybody who appeared to be of Middle Eastern descent. Obviously, just because someone is from Middle Eastern descent, doesn't mean that they are terrorist. But this was a lesson I had to learn the hard way. I remember watching how the media depicted these individuals as evil. I remember feeling scared to even board the

36

plane. I remember sitting in the middle seat between my dad in the aisle and a Middle Eastern man by the window. The Middle Eastern man was nervous the entire plane ride. He was shaking back and forth and looking behind him. It freaked me out. I remember saying to my dadmultiple times, "Dad, something is wrong with this guy. We need to get up. We need to tell someone – tell the pilot. Don't forget those terrorist training videos we saw. We're supposed to get up and alert someone." My dad said, "Justin, shut up! We're fine. Just relax!" But I continued, "No, Dad! He's shaking." I remember the guy getting up three or four times and going to the back of the plane. I kept saying to my dad, "Dad, Dad, what's going on with this guy? Now's the time we need to say something! He's going to come back up here and do something!" Again, my dad told me to relax. Right before we landed, the man went to the back of the plane again and didn't come back to his seat. Once we safely landed, I remember looking towards the back of the plane and I saw him standing with a woman and newborn baby. I assume this was his family he was separated from during the flight and he was anxious not being with them. I felt like such a jerk when I saw that. The reason why he was so nervous and kept going to the back of the plane was so that he could check on his wife and baby. It had nothing to do with him being Middle Eastern or a terrorist – it was him being worried about his family. At that moment, I realizedstereotypes really separate people. Stereotyping puts up barriers that don't allow us to go beyond what we think is true. Stereotypes prevent us from having authentic experiences with one another. I digress – back to the game!

One of the next cards I give out is *Feminist*. Normally, you get someone who is just completely irate and says that men are dogs and that women should take over things. The audience generally confirms that this extreme representation is a feminist. I start the discussion by asking how many people consider themselves to be a feminist. Only a few people raise their hands, so I ask "How many of you are not feminists?" The majority of the crowd raises their hand, so I ask individuals why. I generally

37

hear "Well, I'm not a feminist because feminism doesn't mean being equal to men. It really is an extreme movement and it hurts men." Or I might hear, "I'm not a feminist because being a feminist nowadays doesn't help you if you're a woman of color; it only helps you if you're a white woman." On this particular day, I remember calling on someone who was very eager to explain why she wasn't a feminist. She replied, while popping her chewing gum, "Justin, I am not a feminist because bras are just too expensive!" I gave this woman the craziest look I could muster. She said, "Justin, I'm not going to be going down the street burning my bras. Do you know how much a bra costs at Victoria's Secret?" I immediately responded that I didn't, considering that I've never actually been in the store, let alone purchased a bra. I had to explain to her that the feminist movement has changed over the years. Chances are you're not going to someone on the street burning a bra. Actually, the burning of bras was initially a myth – they were just thrown into a trash can during the 1968 Miss America pageant in protest. Either way, you have to go back to the start with the women's suffrage movement and every wave that happened after. Sure, there may have been some extreme things done, but they were extreme times. Women were trying to gain the right to vote. They were trying to gain the ability to have rights as a person, not as an object owned by men. They were trying to gain the right to buy land. They were trying to gain rights over their own bodies. There were a lot of things to be accomplished over the years. To wrap up this discussion, I asked how many people believe in the equality of everyone. They all raised their hands. I said, "Congratulations! You are all feminists! Give yourselves a round of applause!" The looks on the faces of the crowd are priceless. I see the awe and wonder of them thinking "Wow, maybe I'm not quite sure of the definitions of these words. Maybe I don't fully know these concepts." That is the point of *Stereotype Charades*. It provides a springboard to dive into the definitions and get the meanings out there in a humorous, yet informative manner.

Along with the thought provoking cards we already went

over, another interesting one is *White Woman*. It's funny because normally someone gets up and says, "Oh my God, Becky!" in the most annoyingvalley girl voice possible. In the beginning, a lot of people are yelling out gay person. I always find that interesting because not all people from the LGBTQIA community are flamboyant. Once we get past the fact that it's not a gay person, people usually get it immediately. Like, "Oh my gosh....white girl, it's a white girl!" I recall an example when I did training for over 600 Resident Assistants at a university up north. A young lady got up to act out the card and said, "Oh my God, I totally have to go to Starbucks and I'm wearing UGG boots and my North Face jacket and I have a little dog in my purse!" And no one yelled out "White girl!" like I usually hear. Instead, everyone started yelling out, "Basic, basic, basic!" I'm sitting there dumbstruck and ask what they are talking about? They said, "Come on Justin, you know, basic white girl. Don't you know what that is?" Clearly I didn't and I never had this response before. They go on to explain, "You know, like she walks around really happy. Her hair and nails are always done. She has a little dog in her purse. She wears a North Face jacket and UGG boots. You know...basic!" I had to ask, "Well, how do you become advanced white girl? Is there a test you have to take? If you pass, you become an advanced white girl but if you fail, you're intermediate white girl?" Then silly me as a facilitator, I ask all the women of color in the room, "Is there such a thing as a basic Black girl?" They all angrily respond, "NOPE! And there never will be!" Everybody gets a good laugh out of that.

Since they're all laughing and everything is at a good point, I pose the question, "Where do we get off calling each other basic? When I look around this room, I see unique people with unique figures, sizes, shapes, eye color, hair color, skin tone, and hair texture. When did it become a comedy to call people basic?" People usually respond, "Well, basic is when you're doing the same thing that everybody else is doing; you're not unique." When I hear this, I ask "What do we do with people who don't fit inside the box?" People in the audience start talking and thinking out loud and I hear "Those people are usually ostracized." and "Those people are usually called weird." This really begs the question as to where our priorities lie as a country or as humans in this world. Where do we get off immediately labeling people? Pointing out to them that they are different, that they don't fit in the box with everyone else, thus making them an "other." As a society, we focus so much on social identities that we forget to look at individual personalities or characteristics. We define who someone is based on similarities or differences to the social norm thereby creating a dichotomy. This dichotomy then leaves a distinct otherness – the other being someone who doesn't fit in. They don't fit in because we created a stark difference between "normal" and "odd," and that will always leave people on the outside.

Another interesting topic in *Stereotype Charades* is brought up through the *Handicap* card. Nearly always, the person with this card grabs a chair and pretends they are in a wheelchair. The audiences guess the identity fairly quickly in this scenario. However, one time an actor got up and just stood there. They didn't say anything and they didn't act anything out. This confused a lot of people, but showed a valuable point – not all disabilities are visible. You can't tell if someone has a learning disability, mental health concerns, or if they have a disease or disorder. Again, not all disabilities are seen. Some people even think that individuals with autism are completely disabled and try to assign what they can or cannot do. I have to politely correct them and state that when you meet someone with autism, you are meeting *one* person with autism. There is no line that defines all people with autism – we are unique and special.

I challenge people during this part of the program because they use phrasing such as disabled person or handicapped person. No one ever identifies the person first, the focus is on the disability. They are people with a disability or people with a handicap – the personhood comes first. Sometimes, people don't even consider themselves to have a disability, but rather a *different* ability that doesn't define them. I have a friend with a hearing disability, but he believes that he

40

has a gift and not a shortcoming. He believes he was specially chosen to be part of the Deaf community. The more I learned from him, the more I learned about the Deaf community. Having a hearing loss is not the short end of the stick, but the beginning of limitless possibilities in this community.

Identity is a reflexive process. We call forth one another's identity in part by our conversations with and about one another. To a certain extent we are who the world expects us to be. We become one another's expectations; expectations formed by the power of our words to construct identity. We shape how people view themselves. We shape as how they come to terms with their reality by how we refer to them and treat them. My understanding of people with disabilities came through the eyes of my older brother who was born with cerebral palsy. He was permanently wheelchair bound. He couldn't walk by himself, feed himself, clothe himself, or even speak. Therefore, it was up to us, as a family, to pitch in and take care of my brother. He was more than just a brother to me, he was my best friend. I saw firsthand how people who had disabilities were treated. Again, my brother having a disability was normal to me because that is how he always was. If nothing else, I had no idea something was wrong until we went out in public. People would stare, laugh, and even sometimes point in ridicule. It was then that I realized, "Wait a minute something's not right here! What's wrong with my brother?"

Growing up with my brother taught me many different things, one of the biggest was patience. It taught me to be empathetic with those who had disabilities. It taught me that communication isn't always through spoken or written words – it's also trying to experience life the same way another person does. So, I don't have a problem talking with people who are Deaf. I don't know sign language, but I am going to seek to connect with them. I don't have a problem communicating with someone who is blind and I don't have a problem with someone's inability to walk. We communicate by simply stepping out of our comfort zone and into the comfort zone of another. It is simply a choice.

I thoroughly remember the summer Pokémon Go came out. It was a very popular mobile app at the time and everybody had it. I remember playing everywhere, even one day at the edge of a field. There, I saw a young lady also playing Pokémon Go, but she wasn't going into the field. I assume this was because she was in a wheelchair and ground was rocky and the grass was thick. She looked so frustrated and I think she was going after the same Pokémon as me. I asked her, "Hey, are you looking for that Charmander?" She replied, "Yeah, but I can't get out there." I asked her, "Why?" She said, "Because I'm in a wheelchair, duh!" Really, I wanted to show her that I hadn't just seen the wheelchair, but that I saw her. In the end, I took both our phones into the field and found that Charmander for both of us!

Next, is the *LGBTQIA* card. I've heard, "Oh my God!" and "Hey girl!" I've also seen the person acting out this card walking with their hands on their hips or grabbing someone of the same sex. Because most of the US populations are cisgender and heterosexual individuals, most of the participants are as well. Thus they base their understanding of the LGBTQIA community on the media or their personal experiences. This card is usually guessed very quickly. It's interesting when we have to break down those stereotypes, especially when it comes to the *Trans* card because people often have incorrect preconceived notions about the LGBTQIA community. It's fascinating when I return to Coatesville, PA, my hometown, and see a friend I grew up with. In the course of our conversation, he might compliment me but immediately follows that compliment with the phrase, "No-homo." Essentially, he's saying "I want to compliment you, but I also want to remind you I'm not gay. Even though we've been friends since the age of twelve and you already know my sexual orientation just in case you forgot, please let me remind you every single opportunity I get that I am not gay." The phrase "no-homo" is actually a barrier that implies, I want to compliment you, but I also don't want you to misinterpret my compliment as a come-on because gay is bad, and I am good. I try to challenge my friends by saying, "Hey man, what if I said this to you? 'You lookin' real nice in that suit, no-negro.'" Then they realize "no-homo" doesn't make any sense at all; just like saying, "that's so gay" or "that's so retarded." We have to learn to use words precisely. There are so many adjectives and verbs in the English language that can describe something we don't like. I am here to tell you "gay" or "retarded" are not those words.

Besides the phrases "no-homo," "that's so gay" and "that's retarded," I'm hearing another word that highly concerns me on our college campuses. I often ask students how their day is going. Sometimes they respond that "the day is raping them" or that a test "totally raped them." Using the word rape in everyday conversation like this trivializes the trauma of rape. Casual and frequent misuse of the word rape minimizes its horror and normalizes the word to have a different meaning. If this trend continues, the definition will change – people may no longer perceive it as a violent assault or traumatic experience. The culture of sexual assault on college campuses and society in general is perpetuated by how we label it. Far more apt words can be used to describe a bad day than the word "rape."

"Queer" is also a word that is used differently than its original definition intended, though not in a destructive way. People in the LGBTQIA community have reclaimed this word – they have taken ownership and removed the derogatory connotation. Actually, it is likely that someone in LGBTQIA community will use "queer" over "homosexual." One reason being that term "homosexual" creates a dichotomy – either homosexual or heterosexual, as though there are only two choices. However, sexual orientation is fluid and can change throughout life, but also a person can identify in multiple ways beyond homosexual. This leaves people in the community to not find the word homosexual appealing or appropriate because it is limited. Creating and embracing a diverse community starts with respect for difference, which is nurtured by open dialogue and learning about other cultures and identities.

Unfortunately, I sometimes attend conferences and workshops that aren't very good. I also like to go to workshops that are going to be controversial so I can bring up some

43

interesting concepts. I remember going to a workshop called, *Transgender, the New Phenomenon*. I recall just staring at the programming workbook as I was deciding what programs I wanted to attend and I was thinking, "Really, the *new* phenomenon?!?" As if people just automatically started becoming Trans yesterday like it was a new fad, like a fidget spinner. Yes, it might be more prevalent now because individuals have found the strength to come out, but it's not new. It's important to note that there's a difference between transgender and transsexual, just like there is a difference between gay, queer, asexual, and so on. You have to know the terms and know what you are talking about. That's also important if you're going to speak about a different culture, ethnicity, religious group, or sexual orientation; you have to have friends, be educated, and be an ally. Being an ally is a call to action; it's a movement and it's being in the community. Sometimes, it's knowing when to speak up and when to step aside. It's knowing you can't speak on those experiences, but instead have to encourage the voice of another. Sometimes you can be the best support system by just being there and not saying anything at all. Usually the person who's the loudest in the room isn't the smartest. It's the individuals who are sitting back, listening, and taking account of what is happening who have plenty of beneficial things to say.

As a Preacher's kid, I realize being a LGBTQIA ally might be controversial to some. From my perspective as a Christian man, I'm not responsible for what people do in their life and I am not a judge how they live. Instead, I have to worry about what I'm doing in my life. I value everyone and respect their identities. Who they love does not change their worth to me. My problem in this area is getting people to want to come to church because of their past experiences were so negative. People ask me, "Well how can you be a Christian and support LGBTQIA rights?" I respond by saying, as a Christian, I am called to love everybody. I am called to love everybody, no matter where their life has taken them or who they love. For me to say one group is worse than another would make me a hypocrite and that wouldn't make me a very good Christian, would it? That's why my stance is that – I am a Christian and I am called to love everyone, period.

The next card I'm going to explain is not controversial so much as misunderstood, the *Veteran* card. Once when a participant got this card, they began shouting and screaming unintelligible sounds and words, not making any sense. To me veterans are people who go out there and risk their lives to protect our liberties and freedom. That day, there was a veteran in the audience. He said, "I can't believe you think that! I didn't go overseas, away from my family, and fight so that you could think I am crazy. I was fighting for this country as whole, yet when I was away, this country started taking away the rights of my wife and daughter. That is not what I was fighting for." Reflecting on this, we see that we have dedicated men and women who are fighting for our freedom each day. Yet, when they return, they are not respected and even ostracized because of the psychological effects of war. Even more so, as this veteran described, they are off fighting for a country that doesn't value their loved ones on home soil.

Up next is the *Nerd* card again. At this point in the activity, the audience does not know that I have secretly slipped in two *Nerd* cards (muah haha). As a participant acts out their rendition of the card, the audience looks puzzled but again starts yelling out the words geek, and nerd. I usually put my meanest face on and ask everyone what they are doing. Everyone usually looks guilty and says, "We are just playing the game." I then say to the audience, "Didn't we already learn about this stereotype? It's wrong isn't it? But literally, five seconds later, you revert right back to the same thing!" That's the revelation I want people to realize. We have to un-program ourselves and learn to unlearn.

We finally get to the most controversial card out of all of the cards – *White Male*. I recall giving a *White Male* card to a white male once. Talk about an open book test. He looked at me and said, "Justin, I don't know how to act this out." I said, "Man, just act it out the best way you can." He said, "Dude, I don't

45

know how to do this." I told him to try his best. He gets up in front of the room, looks straight out into the audience, takes a deep breath and says, "I'm normal." The whole crowd went wild. They were shouting, "What does that mean?" and "That's terrible!" while continuing to mutter. My question to every audience that I ever speak to is, "Was he wrong?" When you think about the American Dream, you think about the two-story house with two garages, a pool in the backyard with a swing set for the 2.5 children to play on. You think about the man who runs his own business and a woman who stays at home with the children, waiting for her husband to come home so she can take care of him. When you think about that American Dream, did you think of someone who is Black, someone who is Asian, or someone who is Latinx? No, you only really thought of people who are white and that was this kid's normal.

It's always interesting depending on who is in the audience at the training or workshop. I did training at Lincoln University, which is one of the first HBCUs (Historically Black Colleges or Universities) ever created. The training was for all Black males. Of course, someone had to get the *White Male* card. The person got up and said, "Well, I guess I got to go buy some New Balance shoes!" The crowd laughed hysterically. We, of course, interpret stereotypes within the context of our own life experiences.

Overall, when we define stereotypes, the students and I usually conclude that stereotypes are based on a kernel of truth, but they're not absolutes. We can only really understand others' perspectives once we interact with those who are different than us. So you, the person reading this book right now, are you engaging in conversations with people who are different from you? When was the last time you ate with someone you didn't know or someone of a different race? Would you invite them into your home or introduce them to your family? Would you go to their house or participate in their religious or cultural events? At the end of the day, you have to ask yourself, "Am I truly attempting to understand people who are different than I am or am I fake?" If your answer is, "I'm cool with everybody," but at

46

the same time, there's something about "that person" that makes you feel uncomfortable (and everybody has those feelings, including me) you're pretending. You have to move past those feelings in order to break barriers and build bridges. Talk to someone different – you might surprise yourself. Break down your walls – learn to be comfortable with being uncomfortable and push forward.

Chapter 4
Is That White Privilege I'm Smelling?

You can tell by the chapter title, this is going to be a controversial topic – white privilege. You might think I'm biased because I am a man of color, but I always try to give my honest views on both sides of any particular issue. That being said white privilege is a systematic framework that allows some people to have better and more opportunities, solely based on the color of their skin. This often is related to societal and educational privileges that benefit individuals who are white, or appear to be white. But, do I think that ALL white people are privileged. Absolutely not! I don't think white people wake up in the morning, look in the mirror, and say, "Yes! Still white!" No, it doesn't happen like that. Just like Black people don't wake up in the morning and think, "Aww man, still a minority!" A great comparison to aid with understanding white privilege is to look at Mario Kart. You can't be in first place and also get the blue shell – the players in the back need that to reduce the gap. White privilege is just like that, the people in the front tend to get more opportunities even though they are already ahead of the others. This increases the space between the front and the back. In reality, those in the back need the blue shell, chain chomp, a star man, Bullet Bill, and so on. They need the resources and opportunities, so that they can catch up in society. We need to make sure everyone has the resources to succeed. I've seen it my whole life as a Black man, but I've also seen some white people who use white privilege to benefit others. In the area where I grew up, my best friend is a tall, white, Irish, male with a giant red beard named Shamus. We've been best friends since we were in sixth grade. We've learned so many things about each other growing up, so I definitely can understand some aspects of living in this world as a white person. I can't understand all of it, just like not everyone would be able to understand my position as a Black man. So, for me to sit here and say that every single white person is privileged is absolutely false.

I hear people say, "White people do this." or "Black people do that." What we should say is, "*Some* white people do this." or "*Some* Black people do that." But in the end, it's not even about race. We are all so much more than one aspect of our identities. That is not to say one aspect of our identity is not more salient than another, but that it is not everything we are. In fact, we sometimes invalidate other people's experiences by either speaking for them or saying something that silences them. I clearly remember one time being told by someone who was white, "No Justin, I don't know why you feel that way; it didn't happen like that." We have to be careful to not invalidate people's experiences just because those experiences didn't happen to us personally or affect us personally. The key here is how it affects that person, because it is about that person's experience, not how the other person perceived that experience. Keep in mind that it's not just white people who misspeak. As I mentioned in a previous chapter, if you don't identify with the subgroup mentioned, it's best to be quiet. One of the activities that people play all the time in diversity programs, which I don't care for, is a game called *Cross the Line*. In *Cross the Line*, diverse groups of people stand in a line and are asked a series of questions. If the question applies to them, they move forward, if it doesn't apply to them, they move back. For example, "If you had books in your house, please step forward; if you didn't, please step back." Another common one is "If your parents had jobs move forward; if they didn't, step back." Even something like "If you went on family vacations, step forward; if you didn't, step back." The different questions revolve around social economic status, racism, access to higher education, and so on. In most cases, the white people end up stepping forward to show how privileged they are and the minorities are moving back. Or in a particular case, a question such as, "Has anyone in your family ever been subject to drug use?" and somebody from a minority background steps forward. At this point, people in the back are usually whispering, "Oh my gosh, I didn't know Darryl had to go through that!"

The game is supposed to highlight privilege, but I think it has an adverse effect as well – it highlights those who have had more difficulties in their lives. *Cross the Line* is more often than not a game that exposes those who are economically and socially underprivileged. Statistically, minorities are more likely to fall in this category than those in the dominant culture. So while those in the dominant culture might feel "white guilt," those on the other side of the line might feel embarrassed or even ashamed. No one learns anything except that the activity they have just participated in makes them feel badly about themselves. *Cross the Line* highlights issues we're already aware of without providing solutions.

I've altered this activity to create a game that yields positive results. I made up a questionnaire with all the same questions. The difference is that it is taken anonymously. After participants fill out the questionnaire, I collect them, shuffle them, and redistribute them to different people. This is important for a couple of reasons. First, I want to give individuals the opportunity to walk in someone else's shoes. This helps participants come out of their own experiences and backgrounds.Ultimately it allows them to see through another person's eyes. Secondly, the game allows individuals to go through the simulation without fear of being judged or fear of outing themselves. The participants only know that there is someone in the room who is going through this or has experienced this, but the identity remains secured. The processing of this modified game is very different when it comes to understanding privilege. Now, individuals are looking around the room at each other thinking there's someone in the room that didn't have some of the things they did such as books, clean water, or a private education. They learn someone in the group has gone through struggles or hardships such as a parent who is an addict or who has been in jail, but that person's identity is protected. So, we are able to see that these issues exist, that this has been someone's experience, but the spotlight isn't on that person, it is on the sheet of paper.

The result is that participants understand more clearly

50

where they stand on the continuum of privilege and how this privilege might have given them a head start towards the success we're all seeking. Quite recently, I facilitated diversity training about white privilege. I was sitting next to a white woman who was huffing and puffing the entire time, making noises like she was just disgusted with the topic of white privilege. Finally, I asked her if she was okay and she said, "Yes. I just feel guilty." I asked her what she meant and she replied, "Well, this guilt is just a result of the racist treatment that minorities have to suffer due to my race!" She looked me right in my face, with tears in her eyes and said, "Justin, I am so sorry for my whiteness!" I looked at her and said, "Okkkaaayy?" She said, "No, no, no, I just, I just want you to know that I don't see you as a color; I just see you as Justin." I looked her right in her face and said, "Really? Because every morning I wake up and look in the mirror, I know I'm Black!" It would be really funny to me to see what she would do at a traffic light.

The point of this story is not to trivialize feelings of white guilt but to highlight that we really need to go beyond this color thing. Is there a privilege to being Black? For most people, the concepts of societal advantages for being Black are little to none. But to me, there are some benefits of being Black. It is not just Black and white people who are at odds with one another. If during a program, I ask "If you don't identify with being Black or white, please stand." You can see that there are individuals who don't identify as these races, yet they are not brought into the conversation. These individuals are not consulted about how they feel because we are so focused on the divide between Black and white. When we don't give other individuals a choice, it again, puts us back into this black or white dichotomy. We have to look at the gray area and get everybody's perspective.

I asked this in a previous chapter, but how many of you are intentional about creating and having a diverse experience? About living out the value of diversity? Whether it's with your students, coworkers, staff, friends, or family? How many of you are determined to try different foods, travel to a different country, or learn about a different culture? If you're not intentional about living out the value of diversity, you're not taking full advantage of what this world has to offer. Some people think this country is divided. Some people think this country is a melting pot. I, on the other hand, think this country is a salad! It has vegetables, fruits, herbs, nuts, and different colors, textures, shapes, and tastes. We need to be able to appreciate all of those things.

As a student affair professional, I sometimes get very interesting calls from some of my colleagues. I don't know if they know they are doing this, but I definitely call some of them out on it when it's necessary.

Here's what some of the calls sound like:

[Ring, Ring, Ring.]

Justin: Hello.

Colleague: Hi Justin! How are you? (Extremely high-pitched voice, kind of nervous)

Justin: I'm doing well. How are you?

Colleague: Great! Great! Great! Hey listen, I have this student that I know you'd be great in mentoring! Oh my gosh, this student would really benefit from your leadership and knowledge (extremely excited, high pitched voice).

Justin: Uh huh.

Colleague: Do you mind if I send them over? Like, would that be okay? (Nervous and high pitched voice)

Justin: Yes, of course. Go ahead and send them over.

Colleague: Thank you Justin! You're the best!

Justin: Uh huh. Bye.

Now, in my mind, and in your mind right now, what do you think is taking place? Do you think a student is just going to benefit from my knowledge and experience? Now sure, sometimes that could be the case, but most of the time, it's not. When we talk about intentionality versus intent, we have to look at what's really being said here. In this situation, you know the intent is to butter me up to handle a potentially difficult student. However, I know the intentionality to be that the person coming to see me is a student of color. Low and behold, five minutes later, a student of color walks in my office. Is it because we as student affairs professionals don't know how to challenge and support all of our students? Is it because we don't want to deal with issues regarding students of color – as if their issues are different than any other student? All students, all people, want to be heard and accepted for who they are. If you're floundering, start there. As a Black student affair professional, I have to challenge and support white students. I don't call my white colleagues and say, I have a student you would be a great mentor for – they're white and you're white, so boom, make magic happen! That's not a conversation that I have or that any of us should be having. We have to look at the intent versus the intentionality because as a student affair professional, you didn't hire me because I was Black, at least I hope not. In some cases, at some institutions, that actually does happen. When you're hiring professionals that happen to be of color, you're not just hiring a Black face you're also hiring a Black voice. If the voice makes you feel uncomfortable, go with that feeling, there is probably a lesson coming your way that you need to hear. I'm encouraging everyone, regardless of color, to use their voices to speak out about social injustices. Use your voices to speak out if you see issues of inequality that are not only happening within our communities but on our campuses, in our religious establishments, in our households, and ultimately, in our nation. Our voices share our experiences. Our voices support each other. Our voices raise awareness. Our voices challenge stereotypes.

53

Our voices call attention to the changes we need in our society.

There are just some things white people don't have to go through and can't conceptualize. As I mentioned before, growing up, I had friends of all different races and backgrounds. You have to assimilate and adapt to whatever community you're in. I remember telling my white friends how I grew up and they just couldn't believe it. I asked them, "What did your parents tell you when you were growing up and went into a store?" My white friends had no idea what I was talking about. I told them, "When I go into a store, as a Black male, I have to worry about making sure the clerk sees me immediately and sees that my hands are out of my pockets. If I'm not buying an item, I know not to pick it up. I make sure I'm friendly, smile, keep my hands at my sides, don't make a lot of noise, don't run around, and don't look suspicious. These are the things my parents taught me." My white friends couldn't understand and questioned me, "What? Why would you have to worry about those things? If you didn't do anything, you have nothing to do worry about?!? Right, Justin?" Those are the things as Black men we have to learn and carry with us. I don't necessarily think it's the fault of all white people for not understanding this. These are not things that you think about, so why worry about them?

For example, most of you reading this book are not diagnosed with cancer. So, on a daily basis, you're not thinking about cancer. Why? Because you don't have to! It's the same thing with individuals of color. You're not of color, so you don't think about issues that people of color deal with every day. Let's look at another example – you are driving your car and get pulled over by the cops. As a white male, chances are you're wondering what you did wrong, but you're not fearful for your life. Every time I see a cop, my heart races. But I'm a Black man, I'm supposed to be strong, I'm supposed to be fearless! Those are traits of Black men right? No! When I see a cop my heart starts beating quickly because I don't know what's going to happen. I don't know if this is going to be the last time I breathe or talk to my parents. This isn't even solely based upon what you see in media. This is based upon experiences that I've had personally. I grew up in an all-white neighborhood for the latter part of my childhood. My family moved when my youngest sister was born. We were the second of the houses built in our development. All of the other houses were built after we moved in. I remember whenever we would see any of our new neighbors, who were all white, they would all say, "Hi! Welcome to our neighborhood! When did you move in?" We would just blankly stare and think, "No! When did YOU move in? We were here first!" I can't tell you the number of times my family and I were pulled over in our own neighborhood! Pulled over on the way to work! Pulled over on our way to church! Then, have to prove to the police that we live right there...that's our house! When do you ever have to prove that you live somewhere?

But the fear part is important. Has a cop ever shot at me? No. Have I ever been falsely arrested? No. But you have to look at transgenerational trauma – the trauma that is transferred from the first generation to the current offspring. It's very similar to post-traumatic stress disorder reactions. Can you think of anything that has happened in American history that could cause Black people to not trust people who are white? What about the indigenous people who lived here before anyone else? Do you think they have suffered from transgenerational trauma?

We have to keep in mind many white people don't understand or even realize some of the things that people of color go through. When you're well-spoken as a white male, does anyone ever compliment you on your ability to speak effectively? No! I can't tell you how many times I have been complimented and praised because I happen to sound "articulate." It *almost* comes off as a compliment, but it has a sense of being underhanded, hence microaggressive. Throughout my education, I recall a lot of my professors commenting on how "well-spoken" I was. I'm sure some of you reading this are thinking, well maybe your professors were just complimenting you? But I counter and ask, maybe they could have just told me I did a good job! "Good job" would be a normal response, but as a Black man, I'm told, "You speak so proficiently." or "You speak so eloquently." Those types of compliments are different. They

55

don't come off as praise. If anything, they come off as insults because I defy their expectations of what a Black man is supposed to sound like! Aww c'mon, Justin, you're being too sensitive...maybe you're taking it the wrong way! If you thought this, let's talk again about validating others experiences. What I've explained is how this experience made me feel – this is how I perceived it and how it affects me.

Growing up, I felt like I had to be twice as good as my white peers just to be accepted. In high school, I was in AP classes and I didn't see many people that looked like me. Out of my class of 24, there were only three students of color, when in fact the school was 40% students of color. In college, I didn't see many people who looked like me either. My undergraduate cohort of 65 students only included twelve students of color. In student leadership groups, I didn't see many people who looked like me. In my graduate program, I saw no one who looked like me! When I think about my professors, through all six years of college thus far, I've only had two professors who were people of color. When you don't see people who look like you in the different aspects of your life, it can be difficult. You learn to assimilate so that you can bridge the gap that makes you an outsider. You do this so that you can be seen as an equal, a counterpart, and are valued as a member of the group.

The way I act with my friends, behind closed doors, is not how I act when I'm working in the office because it is not the atmosphere or culture of the workplace. For other people who blend in with the majority, how many times do you have to change your personality or behavior to accommodate your immediate social environment? Some aspects of our identity are invisible or can be hidden. But as a Black male, the color of my skin automatically sets me apart. Thus assimilating with my social environment is not just to fit in, but is absolutely necessary for my very survival. Again, this chapter isn't to say that ALL white people are prejudiced because I don't believe that. Some of my best friends are white! Historically, not all white people were slave owners. There were white people helping in the Underground Railroad. Not everyone in the 1960s was pro-

56

segregation. There were white people who joined the Freedom Rides and were at the Million Man March. When the Black Lives Matter movement happened, there were white people participatingalongside Black people. White people are not the enemy! Unfortunately, from a historical perspective, many white people were pictured as the villains, but in reality, only some were.

When it comes to privilege, unfortunately, some white people are the only ones benefiting. Again, privilege is when you think something is not a problem because it's not a problem for you personally. I do feel that white privilege is something that has to be talked about. You can't just have white privilege and put it in your backpack. You have to check your privilege and the bigotry that goes with it; it is just something that we have to learn to make our society better. We all have to do this, not just white people. Anyone who identifies with a majority class – race, ethnicity, sexuality, gender representation, and religion– has to work towards checking their privilege. It is not automatic and it has to be actively done. Unfortunately, in our society being a cisgender, heterosexual, white, Christian male holds the most privilege and some abuse it. Look at our current political climate where these men are not checking their privilege because if it is not a problem for them, it's not a problem at all! We have to be able to look at it from both perspectives – as someone who has the privilege and someone who doesn't. And we need to call attention to it so that as a society we can re-learn and grow.

If you still don't think white privilege exists, then congratulations! You're enjoying the benefits of it. It does exist and it's something that really does separate our society. As I mentioned before, one aspect of white privilege means that you can be "articulate" and "well-spoken" without surprising others with your ability to speak. If you grew up with white privilege, you didn't have to learn the sad reality of systematic racism. Even when we talk about white privilege, we think about different tragedies that occurred. We think about the Titanic sinking and they say, "Never forget the Titanic!" Or we think about the Twin Towers falling and they say, "Never forget

57

9/11!" Or when they talk about the wars our country has fought there are only white soldiers depicted – as if there were never any Black soldiers in the wars – and they say, "Never forget the war and the lives lost!" But then we look at slavery and you don't hear, "Never forget slavery!" Instead, we always hear, "Get over it!" or "That was a long time ago, haven't we moved on?" It is a privilege or even beyond privilege to erase the atrocity and tragedy of slavery as just something in the past to "get over." White privilege means you talk about Hitler in history class. He killed over 10 million Europeans, but you conveniently skip over Leopold, who was responsible for killing over 15 million Africans. White privilege means you don't have to explain why cultural appropriation is wrong. Think about Cinco de mayo parties, which are used as an opportunity to wear sombreros, ponchos, and mustaches while drinking margaritas and eating tacos. Or rap parties where people dress up like their favorite artist and wear Blackface. Again, this is not a good idea. You don't see Black people dressing up like white people to have a party. Yeah, you do see that in the movie *White Chicks*, which is one of my favorite movies because it's hilarious. We all know everyone's favorite part is, "Making my way downtown…" But, it really doesn't happen that way except in a comedy movie. I know a lot of fraternities and sororities have Fiesta Night and students dress up like a Mexican – or what they stereotype a Mexican to be. That's a problem! We're going to see a Hood Party and everybody dresses up in Blackface, baggy clothes, and act like gangsters. That's a problem! Or think about Halloween and how you would feel if your culture became a costume that makes a mockery out of your heritage, especially when they are embodying harmful stereotypes. That's a problem! We have to be able to call those things out.

Whenever there's a question about Black culture, I'm always the first person everyone looks at, especially when it has to do with hair, skin tone, or clothes. Everybody, not only when I was in school, but throughout my life, always looked to me as if I had all the answers. They would ask, "Justin, can you tell us why Black people do this?" I reply with, "Yes, as the official spokesperson of all Black people in the world, I have concluded..." NO! It doesn't work like that! Everybody is different. My skin color does not determine what I do and do not know – it's all subjective. For my student affairs professionals, this really gets tiresome. It's emotionally and physically draining having to always answer all these questions as a representative of my skin color. It's very easy for you to come to us and ask the questions, but it is also just as easy for you to do the research on your own.

When you're white, no one asks you how you really got that job, got into that school, or got that opportunity. As soon as I walk in, people say, "Wow! How did you land this?" Looking back at my past job searches, I remember changing my voice during phone interviews. Think I'm silly if you want, but people judge you by your name and try to identify you by your voice. If you have a Black name and "sound" Black on the phone, people make conclusions about you. I still remember the looks on people's faces when I showed up in person after a successful phone interview, only for them to find out that I was a man of color. Priceless!

In a similar way, white privilege means you never have to worry about something being called "white-on-white" crime. That term doesn't exist even though there are more white deaths by white hands than there are Black deaths by Black hands. Because Blacks only make up 13.3% of the nation's population, statistically, there are more deaths by white men, yet it's not called white-on-white crime. It's just called crime.

I was able to get an inside view of this white privilege thing when my white friends went off to college. They would frequently tell me stories about how racist people can be, as if I didn't already know. But, my friends were shocked by some of the things other white people said to them. My friends would say, "Well, I think they just assumed I would get it because I was white." One of my white friends I grew up with said he was walking down the street one day at school. There were a bunch of Black students playing really loud music in the quad. He remembered this white guy looked him straight in his face and

59

said, "Hey man! Niggers, right?" He said he looked at the guy and said, "NO! Why are you saying this to me? That is terrible! I can't believe you said that to me!" The guy replied, "Well, they're all like that, aren't they?" And my friend said again, "NO! They are not!" My friend didn't understand because in the community we grew up in, we were taught that wasn't how to treat others. Then he went out into another community, and because of the color of his skin, someone assumed he supported a particular ideology that he did not. You have to recognize, we all use stereotypes all the time, without even knowing it. The enemy of equality is us – it's not other individuals. Take your finger and point at yourself, we are ALL responsible. It wasn't until my friends had their own experiences that they then realized that there are a lot of racist white people in our world. They asked me, "How often do you have to deal with this?" I had to look them right in the eye and tell them, "EVERYDAY!" and they couldn't believe it. We have got to stop labeling people. At one point in time, the world's best rapper was white, the world's best golfer was Black, and the tallest man in the NBA was Asian. We have got to get out of these stereotypes and we have got to be able to really look at things for what they are.

Again, I want to reiterate that I do not think that all white people are racist nor that all white people have the same level of privilege. We also have to look at all of a person's identities and how they intersect. Intersectionality is the interconnection of all different identities – race, religion, sexual orientation, language, ethnicity, ability, and so on. All of these identities play a role in who you are. Yes, some can be more predominant. Yes, some can award you privilege. But some are minority identities as well. Just because a person is white, it doesn't mean they have all the privilege out there. What if the person were a white Trans woman? Or was a white Jewish man with a disability? Or even a woman in and of itself? Each of these identities comes with experiences and voices that need to be heard and valued. Each of these identities make up who we are, and some come with privilege. But we have to remember that identity isn't just skin deep. It is a vast intersecting and

60

complex thing that makes us who we are and shapes how we see the world.

After reflecting on privilege, we have to look at the control that privilege creates, whether that be directly or indirectly. The greatest control that the oppressor holds is to the mind of the oppressed. Think about it, they didn't take *salves* from Africa. They took *Africans* and then made them slaves. They were sold, had stock, and had monetary value. Can you imagine a person being worth a certain dollar amount? Or is life all precious? Their languages, religion, culture, and even names were stripped away. This is why I'm so confused when I hear people say the N-word. Now, don't get me wrong, I have used the word in the past, but what I don't understand is why people think the word is okay. I've said it and knew I was wrong while saying it. Most people, due to our political correctness, don't even say the word anymore. Today, it's coded. The N-word has become synonymous to the word thug, boy, or ratchet. If you want to use the word, that's fine, but we need to start pinning the tale on the racist donkey. We can no longer rely on the, "Oh were reclaiming this word." lie that we have been spewing for years. I can't help but think about the last words Emmett Till heard when he was being killed? People, is it worth using?

This part of the book goes out to all white people who actually get it! Especially to all the white people who take the time to really get to know different cultures and to understand the plight of people of color and minorities. The people who actually march with us, people who lend their hand, lend their privilege to help assist, the advocates and allies, and those who actually want to help us. The struggle is not over! Some people recognize their privilege and actually use it to help. It's an invisible, weightless backpack. But everybody carries this thing of privilege whether you have a lot of it or just a little. We have to explore white privilege. If you're white, take a second, have you ever thought about your privilege? Do you benefit from it? Does your privilege inhibit other people from moving forward? We have to start unpacking this invisible backpack called white privilege. Some people may read this chapter and get immediately offended. "Justin, this is an anti-white chapter! How can you say these things?" I want to remind the reader that I am not anti-white. I'm about the progression of everyone. We have to call out our present system and make strides for a better one because being pro-Black doesn't mean being anti-white!

Chapter 5
Perceptions

Cultural perceptions are defined by many different methods. Media, entertainment, and other forms of popular culture create them. They play a significant role in how we view other backgrounds, how we make decisions about what others think, and shapes our outlook. As we talked about in the previous chapter, perceptions shape how we understand stereotypes and contribute to our marginalization of others. We all have issues with perception. Perception can be formed by countless thoughts and is based off of many realities. Unfortunately, that's how we as humans see the world; our reality is our perception. But if we see, hear, and say the same things, would our perceptions be the same or different? Let's try a test. Below, I have a sentence for you to read out loud. Really, read it out loud. Go!

> Funky Frogs are the result of years of scientific research contrasted with the study of years.

Did you read it out loud? Do it again! One more time! Now, I need you to count how many F's you see in that sentence. Go ahead and count. There's no time limit; go ahead and count how many F's you see in that sentence. Did you get it yet? How many did you count? Did you count three? Did you count four? Did you count five? Well, if you counted six, you would be correct. For those who didn't count six, what happened? Was it just your perception? Was it because you went only off what you saw, not what you spoke? And that's the thing with perceptions. Perceptions can really just change the tiniest facet about how we understand concepts. I remember a couple years ago there was a huge controversy about a dress's color; was it blue and black, or was it white and gold? People were staying up late at night trying to figure this out while others actually went to the store to see for themselves. People were arguing that someone had altered the image to mess with people on social media. Scientists were telling us it is due to the retinal cones in your eyes that let light in. It all has to do with perception.

Perception can look like many different things. For example in the US, crickets are considered pests – dirty and annoying. You would be annoyed if you heard crickets chirping all night in your house. However, in northern Thailand, they're actually considered an appetizer or delicacy. I often think about women in the United States who look towards women of the Middle East and think "Everything's covered but her eyes; what a cruel male dominated culture." And then the women in the Middle East are looking towards American women thinking "Nothing covered but her eyes because she has sunglasses on, what a cruel male dominated culture." They're both thinking the same thing, but their perception is very different, and again perception changes how we think about the world. It also depicts how we move through life and how we really gain an understanding.

In the same regards as perception, we have to look at culture. Culture is learned and shared. It's unconscious and dynamic, but our cultural lenses often influence ethnocentric meanings. So where do you get your cultural lenses from? Do you get it from what you're taught – what you learned in school? Do you get it based upon what you have read? I feel like sometimes individuals would rather have a reassuring lie than an inconvenient truth. For example, you would be surprised at the amount of schools that I travel to where individuals still think that Thanksgiving happened the way that they were taught in school. Yeah that's right. There are a lot of people who think that in 1492 Columbus sailed the ocean blue and landed in what is today the United States. We all know, historically, he found this land by accident and that he and his people couldn't survive here. The indigenous people, who already thrived here, helped them cultivate the land and they all had a giant feast for Thanksgiving. That's what a lot of students still perceive to be true. It's not in their mind that these individuals stole that land, raped, murdered, and pillaged entire villages just to declare them their own. We even sing songs about them. And didn't you know, celebrating Columbus Day means you could get 30% off your mattress!

These concepts are very difficult to conceptualize if we only focus on the surface. Let's compare culture to an iceberg – you know icebergs are much bigger at the base and only show a small portion on the surface. This is similar to people; we only see the surface. We see skin color, language, food, and clothing. Because that is all we see on the surface, that is only how we develop our perception of different cultures. But, let's not forget everything underneath the surface that supports these different cultures – values, perceptions, cultural and social norms, communication styles, and so much more. These beliefs are the foundation to what is on the surface that we can see. You'd be surprised at the amount of schools that I spoke at where individuals didn't think that Thanksgiving actually happened that way. You'd be surprised at how many people think the Holocaust didn't happen. There are students that have been taught that the Holocaust was just a distraction during the war, to take different countries off of their game. They truly do not believe it was an actual historical turning point for Jewish people in Germany. Really? I am amazed at the faces of students when I tell them that in Germany, people knew what was going on – people saw their Jewish neighbors being dragged out of their houses and killed. Some of them even robbed their neighbors when their houses were abandoned. How can you think that these historical atrocities did not happen?

I often think about this one professor of mine who asked me, "Justin, why do all the Black students sit in the back of a class? How come they never sit up in the front? You sit in the front." I really had to think about it because as I've said, sometimes individuals want to make you the spokesperson for the entire race. I asked my professor, "Do you think your students of color feel comfortable sitting in the front?" My professor had a puzzled look on his face and said "Well I'm not sure about that." I then said, "You should ask them what they think because sometimes our students, especially our students of a color feel safer to sit in a place where they can find their strength. Because strength in numbers is where their strength emanates from." So if you see a group of students hanging out in a particular section, ask them why is that? Is it because they don't feel that comfortable in the majority or do they feel that they would not be welcomed?

We all know the beliefs are drawn from our own culture's view of reality. To understand culture, you have to look at it through the lens of individual beliefs in order to examine what those beliefs have already created. If you perceive things that may be incorrect from other cultures through your own cultural lens, you may be seeing people through a different set of eyes. I often think about offices of cultural awareness or multicultural affairs at universities. When I go and speak to the directors of those offices, they always say to me, "You know Justin, people always think that our office is the Black office, we never get students who are white to come in, why is that?" It's almost the same thing in reverse of what I just explained. Do you think that your white students would feel comfortable entering this office? Do you make it welcoming for *everybody* to walk inside the door? What are their perceptions and beliefs of this office? These things have to change.

It's the difference between intentionality versus the intention. Sometimes we have to change our own perception for ourselves and develop a new understanding. For example, as a Black male, when I'm walking into a store, I make sure that I smile. I make sure that the clerk sees who I am – that I'm friendly and I'm not present to create trouble. That's not the same way I have to be when I go into the city. I don't have to go around and shake hands and pretend like I'm something that I'm not. If anything, it's the exact opposite when I'm walking through the city. I don't smile at anybody and don't say hello to anybody. Why? Unfortunately, you have to show that you are a tough guy. You have to put on a mean grit or they'll think that you're soft. Being soft in the city can sometimes be a dangerous thing. So as a Black man I have to constantly change who I am

66

to adapt to my surroundings.

As we have discussed, perception is received differently from person to person. But I still get the same old thing when I travel. I often hear people say that we have to give money to Africa because they are poor. That's a very false perception. There are a lot of rich people and rich areas in Africa. Did you know Africa has blue water beaches? Look it up. There are poor areas in Africa just like the poor areas of the United States. So when people say we have to give to the poor over there, I ask why we don't give to the poor here. It's making these perceptions that are incorrect. I remember I had a false perception about celebrities at one point. At the beginning of this book, I told you I met close to 300 celebrities in my lifetime. I had false perception that celebrities were greater than life, not down to earth, or that they were untouchable. It wasn't until I met the late Dr. Maya Angelou that I learned my perceptions were completely incorrect. I remember Dr. Angelou came to visit Slippery Rock University and I was given the very special opportunity to meet her backstage. I sat there doing role-play as to what I was going to say to this woman. I mean, she was a huge icon in my community. My mother owned her books and I remember hearing about her struggles, courage, and insight growing up. I knew I only had a brief amount of time and I didn't want to embarrass myself, so I remember just sitting there contemplating what I was going to say. I rehearsed my lines: "Good evening Dr. Angelou" or "Dr. Maya Angelou, how are you, nice to meet you." Or should I go more casual with a "What's up Dr. A?" No matter what I came up with, I didn't think anything was good enough. I decided that when I met her, I was going to wing it. So I got behind stage and Dr. Angelou was there and, fortunately, I was the first person to meet her. I was so nervous because everybody was standing around watching me. I don't know why I did this but when I went up to her, she extended her hand to me. I grabbed her hand, bowed and said "Nice to meet you." Dr. Angelou looked me straight in the eye and said, "Honey child, the only person you bow to is the great one." and she pointed up as if referring to God. That was a really big day for me to learn about perception.

Our perceptions are our own and you can't go off what people tell you. People want you to accept their beliefs based off of their perceptions and experiences. But, your experiences can be the complete opposite. I always think it's interesting when I'm talking to people who are not of color and they say something like, "You know Black people are still holding on to the slavery thing, like I was never a slave owner, why should I be responsible for this?" or "You know it was my great-great grandfather who did this not me, we should start over." I think it's unfair for people to tell Black folk they need to get over something when people are still walking around with Confederate flags chanting "Never forget the south." Let's think about it this way. Black people are asked to get over slavery so the nation can move on. Yet, we have people in the country holding on to a symbol from a war they lost over the right to own slaves. It truly makes you question which group is the one that needs to move on. And I can tell you, the answer is not Black people.

We have to be able to make sure that our perception is equal. We need to meet each other on an equal playing field so that our realities can almost sync up. For example, I can't understand why Flint, MI still doesn't have clean water and I don't know why we're not talking about it. We'll spend millions and millions of hours talking about the Kardashians or what Donald Trump just did, yet there are people in this country who still don't have clean water. I want you to imagine that for a second. We take so many things for granted, especially here in the US. Imagine waking up and trying to wash your face, you turn on the water, and out comes a sludgy brown substance. Could you survive that way? Could you live that way? Would you complain? Would you be upset? These people have been living like this for over a year and nothing's been changed. I don't understand how we could pay 15 billion dollars for a wall to divide the continent, but don't have 55 million to provide clean water to our citizens. That doesn't make any sense to me.

This conversation always brings up taxes and what our

taxes fund. I am happy to say that I agree with how some of our tax dollars are being used. I think a lot of people out there like NPR and PBS because it provides us with the opportunity to learn and entertainment. These entities take $1.37 out of your taxes to be funded each year. Well guess what, take my $1.37 – I love NPR and PBS. I will gladly pay taxes for the service they provide. Also, $.11 out of my taxes goes to developing minority businesses and $.66 for entrepreneurship and innovation. They can absolutely take $.48 so they can fund a civil rights division of the US Department of Justice. If we're going to be able to defend the planet Earth, give them that $1.38. If they need $9.00 to install safeguards for our climate, take it! I added up all of those costs they're only taking $22.36 out of my paycheck to fund these things a year. Look if all it takes were $23.00 a year to for us to make America great again, wouldn't it be worth it?

So little of our tax dollars are going to things that will protect our planet, both the people and the earth itself. Barely anything goes to the Corporation of Public Broadcasting that helps fund PBS and NPR – entities that educate and connect us to the world around us. So where is all the money going? Is America greedy? Is America privileged? Is America too privileged? Like I said, some people say it's a melting pot. I don't think so – I think it's like a salad with blends with different shapes, textures, and flavors. But let's get back to America. America is supposed to be the land of free and the home of the brave. Are we really free, or are we chained up by our own perceptions of how things should be? Are we stuck in the past or stuck accepting the truths of others? Are we brave enough stand up for others or what we believe in? Can you imagine being in a place without some of the freedoms we take for granted on a daily basis? Even the mere idea of thinking differently than the dominant culture is a death sentence in some places. Yet, we have this ability and we remain silent. We do not correct the negative perceptions. We don't fix the things that need to be fixed. We argue about that $.48 each a year to fund a department for civil rights is a waste of taxpayer money. But, there are people in so many places that want nothing more than the opportunity and the ability to call America their home.

Let's think about the privilege we have here in America. It's hard to argue that we don't have more opportunities and access than many other places throughout the world. But with this, we need to talk about the greed we also have. I think of all the nonprofits and organizations doing things like "Saving Africa." Broadcasting their TV ads about how a $1.00 day could save a child's life. But, where is all that money going? Organizations are collecting this money, but where are the outcomes? Not too long ago, Akon, a popular rap artist, used his own money to provide electricity to over fifty million Africans. Where were those organizations then? Let's also think about how we funnel money to these organizations to "save" Black children in Africa, while we sit here in America and allow Black kids to get killed walking down the street. Of course, I'm not saying to stop donating money to good causes that help those in need around the world; it is very honorable to do if the money is being used appropriately. But why are we sending money to save a Black kid in Africa when we can't stand up and speak out for the Black kid shot playing with his friends in Ohio? Don't worry, we'll get into this more in the next chapter.

I think one of the more important games that I've ever played in D.A.P. (Diversity Awareness Program) was a game called *The Pain Game*. I played this activity during Black History Month and there were about 120 students in attendance that evening. I asked people,"Could you relate to the pain that slaves had experienced?" The individuals that were in the room all said, "Oh no Justin...of course not. I could never be able to recreate that pain. I mean they were being taken away from their families, having their entire cultures and identities stripped from them, killed, raped, berated, and mocked." and "There's no way that we could possibly recreate their pain." But I said, "Despite what pain it may be, pain is pain." That is something that everyone experiences and it is something that connects all people. We talk about aspects that bring us together and our differences, but we never talk about pain. Next, I have students anonymously write their innermost pain or fear on a piece of paper and place them in a bag. I shuffled this up and read some notes out loud. Some of those papers were really noteworthy and I think what was most impactful was the processing that took place after. Some of the fears included: I used to think all Black people were bad until one saved my life; I currently have cancer; Me and my best friend had a falling out and we've yet to get it together and I see my best friend every day; I constantly steal because I'm homeless; I'm in college because my parents are forcing me too...I don't know what to do; My parents are divorcing and they're not thinking about their children.

These small pieces of paper give a glimpse into the hearts of the people in the audience. A room where no one knows each other instantly turns into a productive group counseling session. As I read those notes out loud, I saw people starting to give people hugs, hold hands, show faces of concern, and ultimately show their humanness compassion for others. Sure, some people are probably sitting there asking themselves where did this come from or who is it this person? It even goes through my head when I do these activities. People are putting their life's deepest darkest fears, pains, and secrets on a piece of paper and having them read aloud. It can definitely bring up some type of emotion and evoke some type of reaction. It's interesting to see the commonality of these fears and pains. A lot of them happen to be about poor relationships and how they recovered from them. It is good to know that even with your darkest pain, you are not alone. That someone else is going through something similar or has survived it.

My father always talks about how people who have been hurt end up hurting people. That sometimes you really can't fault people for hurting you because that is all they know. Some people do it intentionally, some people do it unintentionally, but it still happens. People can only meet you as far as they've met themselves. You can't expect people to do something outside of the norm of what they already know. Again, I can only speak from *my* Christian perspective, and I understand that not everybody reading the book is a Christian, but a lot of these notes were about the church. They totally killed me to hear the

71

pain that a church caused to them. One especially stands out to me to this day. It read "I was very welcome in my church until they found out that I was gay." And that's a problem.

When we talk about perceptions, again, we talk about what is right and what is wrong.Perceptions can have a right way and they can have a wrong way. For example, today people say don't break the law, I mean they probably always said that, but there have been some big exceptions. In the past, there were a lot of big laws that were broken. If you sheltered Jews over in Germany, you were breaking the law even though you were saving them from the Holocaust. The Underground Railroad included a lot of individuals who decided to break the law. Harriet Tubman broke the law. Rosa Parks broke the law. If you really want to talk about the creation of our country, the Boston Tea Party broke the law. I think it all depends on how you're looking at a situation. Why didthese individuals risk their lives, livelihood, families, reputation, and their futures just to break the law? Was there something within the perception that had to change? Was it worth going through such extreme means to ensure that individuals were treated fairly and that people's basic civil liberties were upheld? Sometimes when I am at the gym, I see people making fun of bigger people working out. I don't understand that. They talk about them and shame them. You should be happy that people want to better themselves. Making fun of someone who's a little bigger at the gym is like making fun of a cancer patient who's getting chemotherapy. If individuals are doing something to make them healthier or feel better, why do some think it's good idea to shame them? We can always go back to the age-old proverb, "If you don't have anything nice to say don't say anything at all." But we don't live like that. We live in a society where we have the First Amendment and the right to free speech. Therefore, we have the right to say whatever we want whenever we want. No, I don't think so. I think that people hide behind that. Even though you have the right to say whatever you want you also have to be held accountable for the things that you say.

To wrap up the conversation on perception, we must

think of how we are going to move forward. We must reflect on what our perceptions are and how we overcome these to move on for the betterment of society. We've got to have some effective cross-cultural communication. In order to accomplish that, we have to do a few things. We have to build self-awareness. You do this by going to events, researching, learning, and supporting your friends when they're having cultural conversations. We've got to recognize the complexity. You're not going to be able to understand people's culture overnight. You might not even be able to understand it throughout the course of your lifetime, but you have to try. You've got to avoid stereotyping. Stereotypes do nothing but separate us. Even if they are so extreme and almost become comical, they are still harmful. Stereotypes have the potential to give us some insight, but they're not an absolute. We've got to be able to respect other's differences. At the end of the day, I don't have to agree with you but I should respect your opinion and you should respect mine as well. No opinions are wrong that's why it's called an opinion. We need to listen actively. God gave us two ears, two nostrils, and two eyes, but only one mouth. There is significance in that. We need to be honest and ask questions. If you don't know, ask. I repeat, if you don't know, *ask*. That's how you gain the knowledge, but you also have to be honest when you're wrong. It's perfectly fine to say, "Hey, I don't know about this, could you tell me more?" or "Hey, I wasn't sure why I saw you do this, can you give me some more insight?" We have to be flexible, but know that it's not always going to go your way. I'm sorry, but readers, it's not always about YOU! So we've got to be able to think twice when we're having these misconceptions. We have to distinguish the perspectives. What do you know to be true, what do you know to be false, and how does what you know compare to what someone else knows?

Chapter 6
Indeed, Black Lives Truly Matter

Black lives matter or do they? Man, this movement, this call to action, this Black Live Matter thing has truly thrown our society, our nation, and our world into global sensitivity. What does Black Lives Matter truly mean? Does it mean that only Black lives matter? Does it mean that Black lives matter and white lives don't? Is it a hate group? Is it a movement that wants to destroy white power? We could try to take a look at what the media says surrounding this so-called Black Lives Matter, but I'm not sure if we would get much from that view? I have to ask myself what I think about people like me – Tameer Rice, Trayvon Martin, Eric Garner, and Sandra Bland just to name a few, do we matter? What about their families? How do they feel about the situation, and grieve? How do they turn on their TV and have to be reminded about it with multi-media coverage about another slain person of color?And what about me, the author? Today, I could be a public speaker, tomorrow I could be a doctor, but the next day, I could be another hashtag on social media. Does my life matter? Does the life of my future son matter?

All these questions are really puzzling especially when I think about my own experiences in my life. I remember my parents talking to me about college ever since I was a kid. I remember walking to my grandma's house and her asking me "Hey Justin, do you want to go to college one day?" and I told her no because I hated school. I remember my grandmother conveniently going into a cabinet and pulling out an old assignment that my uncle completed when he was my age. The assignment asked him what he did this summer and he said nothing. It asked how many books he read; he said not one darn book. I remember my grandma looking at me and telling me, "You know your uncle also hated school at one time and he went on to get his doctoral degree." And literally, twenty years later, I was graduating with my master's degree with hopes of getting a Ph.D.

But I also remember in ninth grade where everybody went to go meet the school counselor. My counselor called me in and said she wanted to learn more about me. She wanted to get an idea of how I was doing academically and to see what my plans were post high school. I told her that I wanted to go to college and study Psychology. My school counselor looked me right in the face and said, "I'm looking at your grades right now and it doesn't seem like you are college material. Perhaps you want to pick up a trade or a skill? That's going to be really beneficial for you. Maybe cutting hair, doing masonry, or working on cars are more for you. That might be really useful for you in the future." I remember looking at her and saying no, and that I would be going to college. She said that with my grades, it doesn't look like I would get there. Boy was she wrong! This story reminds me how waymany Black youths are treatedin America. They're told that they can't do it. They get robbed of their self-esteem and are told that they're not good enough. They are shown that their ambitions and goals aren't important, and maybe, because of the color of their skin, they are unfit to achieve their dreams. All I have to say is if your dreams aren't scary enough then you're probably not dreaming big enough.

Going back to the main subject, the way Blacks are treated in America is completely unacceptable. It's not always white people who are attacking people of color. People of color attack people of color. With that being said, how many of you would actually like to be treated like Blacks are treated in America? I'll wait while you answer that question...I didn't think so.That's why the Black Lives Matter is a call to action. Let's compare the Black Lives Matter and All Lives Matter because it is such an interesting concept. Is All Lives Matter essentially saying that everyone matters while Black Lives Matter is saying *only* Black lives matter? No, I don't think so. Who in their right mind would say only Black lives matter? That doesn't make sense. Of course, all lives matter! My question is where was All Lives Matter during slavery? Where was All Lives Matter during the women's suffrage movement in the twenties? Where was All Lives Matter when there were Japanese internment camps during WWII? Where was All Lives Matter when the LGBTQIA community was fighting for the right to marry? Where is All Lives Matter now when Syrians are seeking refuge in our country? Where was All Lives Matter during any of these battles? Those individuals always seem to be quiet during these times.

People say that Black Lives Matter is a hate group. They riot, they destroy, they are violent, and they're like the Black Panthers. Well the interesting thing about the Black Panthers is it was group designed to be non-violent. The Black Panthers were designed to *police* the police because the police were taking the law into their own hands; the police were completely being prejudiced against those who were of color. You never heard of the Black Panthers going out and shooting and killing someone. That's not what the group was about. Yet, the KKK, a nationally recognized hate group, is known for and boasts about hanging people of color, killing Jews, and destroying people of a different sexual orientation.But we don't call those groups terroristic.

I'm also hearing things about Blue Lives Matter in references to the police. This movement now focuses on how cops feel like they are in more danger and at risk because of prejudice against them. What's interesting is that when we talk about Blue Lives Matter, it doesn't mean that only cops matter and that everyone else doesn't matter. Blue Lives Matter says cops lives matter and they are representing their uniform. A uniform is something you wear, something you put on to represent that occupation. You can't compare an occupation to the color of someone's skin – his or her natural born race or ethnicity.

If you're really paying attention to the Black Lives Matter movement, if you're looking at that statement, there's almost an invisible *also*, or *too* at the end. So it really says Black Lives Matter Too or Black Lives Matter Also. We are just trying to bring attention to issues surrounding people of color. It doesn't mean any other issues are not important. We're just trying to bring attention to our issues. It's the media – news, Internet, social networking – that makes it seem like this is an all-pro-Black movement. You wouldn't see someone go participate in a save the rainforest campaign and say "Yellowstone Park trees matter also." It wouldn't happen. You wouldn't see someone atRelay for Life, an organization that aims towards helping those battling cancer, say "All diseases matter." They wouldn't do that because of course all these things matter.

What's problematic for me though, as a 27yearold Black male living in a suburban, upper-middle class area, is that I remember the night that the verdict of Trayvon Martin came out. I was so angry that I went out for a run. I remember getting a call from my mom late that night, around 11:30pm. She was upset that I was out at that time of night running, maybe even a little scared. She asked me, at age 27, if I knew what to do if I was stopped by the police. I said, "Of course I know what to do, Mom. It's the police, when they tell you to pull over, you pull over. You turn your car off, put your hands out the window, show them you're not a threat, and show them you don't have any weapons." My mom stopped me right there and said, "No, do you know what to do when the police pull you over?" I was so confused about what my mom was talking about. I said, "Yeah Mom, like the same thing I just said." She said, "No that's not the time for you to show them how educated you are with your master's degree. It's not time for you to prove to them that you live in the area or that you belong on God's green earth. It's the time for you to do whatever they tell you to do so that I can see you the next day." I didn't understand what she was saying. My mom quietly clarified, "Well sometimes in order to keep your life as a Black man, it means you've got to release your dignity, it means you've got to release your humanity, it means you have to forego your entirety as a human being. If they want to spit on your soul, you let them because that allows me to be able to keep you as my son the next day." As a 27yearold man having to hear my mom tell me that just really broke my heart. My mom would rather me go through full humiliation as a person so that she could see me again.

77

Let's look at all the information on Black-on-Black crime. Black-on-Black crime is a myth. It's something that's set up by society, newspapers, and social media to show disaggregated information, which might not even be true. You never hear something called white-on-white crime because it doesn't exist. Why is a Black-on-Black crime even a thing? Maybe it's a thing because people fear Black people. You have no clue how many times I'm walking down the sidewalk at night alone and I see a white couple walking towards me. They completely jump off the sidewalk and walk across the street so they don't have to walk by me – and I'm a teddy bear. There is a true fear of people of color in this country. Is this fear based off of things they see on TV, read in the newspaper, or stories they heard? I have never personally done anything to anybody that would make me scary, so why just run away from me? I can tell you, I've been in elevators where women will clinch onto their purses and shift away from me. It's a very shameful feeling to know that people have these preconceived notions about you before they even get a chance to know you.

I've seen this struggle of Black people my whole life. Most people usually hear "the United States of America...the land of the free." But this place is also called "AmeriKKKa," where people of color are killed for walking down their own street. Shot for holding their wallet when they get pulled over by police. We have Black men being sent to jail for crimes they didn't commit, but are presumed guilty because of the color of their skin. I have friends that are in prison over outrageous and outlandish charges. Skin color is not a reasonable suspicion. But Blacks, still in their best way, most of them maybe, not all of them, try to follow the rules. We are just like every other race of people, some good eggs, and some bad ones. We try to fit in. We try to participate in the marches. We try to make it in this world. So it seems like Black people do fit in, or at least try to. But in America, that's not always in our favor. We're living lives that people can't fathom in their scariest nightmares, yet we're supposed to fit in, fall in line, and do what we have to do. I can't begin to tell you how many times I've seen people say go back to

Africa or go back where you came from. In America, if everybody were forced to go back to where they came from, there would barely be anyone left! Let's not forget that a lot of Americans are multicultural too, where would you go? Maybe half of you would go to Ireland and the other half to Italy? Perhaps a quarter to Thailand, a quarter to Mexico, a quarter to Armenia, and a quarter to Nepal? How does someone tell a Black person to go back to Africa if you're not willing to go back to where you or ancestors came from?

Sometimes when I'm driving through Pennsylvania, I have to go through places called sundown towns – places that were historically dangerous for Blacks when the sun went down – and it's truly terrible. Honestly, you also don't want to be Black going through those towns when the sun is up either. To my readers, I don't know what your background is but there are some places that when the sun goes down you're still okay. You can still walk the streets. You can still drive through and everything will be fine. I know for me, there are just some places that when the sun has gone down, you will not catch me there. I try to get gas before I drive through out of fear that someone's going to stop and ask me why I'm there, or that police will pull me over for just for existing. You may run into someone that will want to do a mandatory search or if I go to a place to get food, they can just refuse to serve me and not even tell you why. These are areas that keep me scared. These places were really prevalent in the south but they still exist today. They exist everywhere.

Unfortunately, to be relatively conscious and Black means to always be angry. It's strange because if you're "woke" as they say, you can really get sucked into what that truly means. You would be angry all the time because of the injustices that you are constantly facing. The constant battle that you have to fight every day to prove that you're supposed to be a part of this great nation. You have to prove that you're worthy of your degrees, that you're allowed to be in the same classes as other people, and that you earned your job. There are times I felt I had to keep quiet. That being quiet was the best way for me to be able to get through and survive. Keep your head down, say nothing, and do what you got to do. No matter if I was outspoken or I was quiet, I went through the same experiences.

I just look at individuals like Tameer Rice – a twelveyearold kid who was shot because he had a BB gun in a park. I asked some of my white friends when they had gotten a BB gun; most said around nine years old. I asked them if they ever played with the gun in the park. For them, that was a common place or out in the woods. I can't imagine any cops shooting them down. What kind of training takes place where several cops have to kill a twelveyearold over a BB gun? There was no communication. There was no "Get on the ground!" There was nothing. Shoot first, ask questions later.

I used to laugh when my dad asked me what I wanted to be when I grew up. I would tell himwanted to be a Psychologist. My dad would say, "Wouldn't you want to be president one day?" I would just laugh because at that point in my life I hadn't seen anybody who looked like me as a President of the United States. In fact, they made a very funny movie about that in 2004 called *Head of State* starring the famous comedian Chris Rock. He depicted how it would be in America if a Black man ran for president and he won in the end. A very comical movie, but the movie was made because no one in their right mind would ever picture that a Black man would be Commander-in-Chief or leader of the free world. It wasn't until 2008 when Barack Obama was elected President, that maybe, we as a people were able to come up. Maybe those dreams and aspirations weren't too big, maybe we had broken through the glass ceiling. I remember everyone being excited, including me, on election night thinking "Man, he did it! Man, this country's going to be different. Man, we're really going to come up after that." Then I think about our reality, we elected a president that we did not allow to do a thing. Sometimes, the only thing that we allowed Obama to do was to break the color barrier. His hands were tied during his entire presidency. We moaned. We complained. We held him up. People talk about all the great things that Obama did, and I agree I think he did marvelous things. The things that keep me up at night are wondering what else he could have done

80

if we just let him. What barriers could he have broken down? How much farther could we have been as a nation if we truly just allowed him to do the things that he needed to do? Now, because I'm saying that doesn't mean that I'm pro-Obama. I'm just saying that facts are facts. When people are talking about opinions and they say, oh well he did this and he did that. However you feel about a candidate it doesn't matter. What matters is the outcome – all which was achieved to better our country.

So right now, in this current time, we have Donald Trump as our president. I'm not saying I'm for Trump, not saying I'm against Trump. You should never be against your Commander-in-Chief. That's like being against your own airplane pilot. Some people don't like the pilot. Well guess what, we're all on this plane right now and we need to get there together. So, regardless of if you like your pilot or not, you need to support him so we can make sure that we get to where we need to be. I remember my father always telling me I could be the President of the United States and me just laughing about it. I never realized that it was something I could actually accomplish until 2008. But think to yourself, how many things have you been able to accomplish that you thought were impossible?

Are there things out there that you would like to do that you haven't? Don't have dreams, have plans! What are your plans and aspirations and are you truly working up to your fullest potential to meet them? I never thought that I would have two businesses. I would never have thought that I'd be writing a book. There have been a lot of setbacks in my life, but failure only comes when growth is right around the corner. You can't expect to grow without having a little bit of failure in your life. Do you expect everything in your life to work out fine? That's simply not going to happen because life doesn't work that way. It's always a roll of the dice and you have to play the hand that you've been dealt. Look, at one point in my life, my life could have been described as Jason Peele's horror film, *Get Out*. But that's another story, for another book, at another time.

My biggest question about all these terrible events we hear about daily is whether or not these actions had to be lethal.

Yes, I understand the police have to report to the situations. Again, we talk about Tameer Rice, a twelveyearold kid who was shot by the police. The police couldn't call over to him and asked if that was a toy? They couldn't tell him to stop, drop the gun, or toss it over to them? He was twelve, he was a child. The police didn't have enough training not to shoot and kill this kid? I think about Trayvon Martin and the George Zimmerman verdict. It doesn't matter how you feel about the verdict. It doesn't matter how you feel about George Zimmerman. We've got to look at the facts. Facts say that when George Zimmerman called it in as a situation, he was told to not pursue this child. He should have listened to the orders of the authorities. Therefore, by not following those orders, he failed to comply. Anything he did after the fact, he should have been held accountable for. He shot and killed a child. Let's think about Eric Garner. A lot of people say you can't talk about Eric Garner because he was illegally selling cigarettes. You know what, that may be true but was it a crime worthy of a death sentence? That's my question to all these cases. Even if George Zimmerman had beaten up Trayvon Martin, I would rather him be bruised than shot and killed. I would rather all of these people have been beaten up rather than shot and killed. My question remains, why is it always lethal? I know that police officers have taser guns but I rarely see them used. They always use bullets when it comes to us. I don't even get it.

Some of these videos have even gone viral. I remember seeing one unarmed Black man shot almost 28 times in a video last year. Osama Bin Laden didn't even get shot 28 times! But, Black men are shot that many times? I don't get it. It doesn't make any sense and that's why people of color react the way they do. I hear people say "All I see is Black people rioting destroying their own cities and it's horrible. They should think of something more constructive to do instead of all this rioting. The rioting isn't doing anything." Okay, so Black people should have peaceful protests. When I think about peaceful protests, I think about Martin Luther King and all those unarmed people in the 60s, and what happened to them? Canines were released on them. They had hoses sprayed on them. They had their cars set on fire. So maybe we shouldn't have peaceful protests. Maybe Black people should just remain quiet and not say anything. Okay, so let's think of this past 2016 NFL season and Colin Kapernick, remember him? All he did was take a knee before a game. Look at all the controversy and the criticism he faced for not putting his hand over his heart during the national anthem. This was a silent and peaceful move to bring attention to an issue. And he was a proven winner who took his team to the Super Bowl. Yet, no one in the NFL wants to even hire him now. Now you're telling me that Black people can't riot. They can't speak up, they can't sit down, and they can't peacefully protest. What's left for them to do? Maybe they should wait quietly and rely on the judicial system, because it's innocent until proven guilty, right? Wrong! If you haven't seen the Netflix documentary *13th*, you should catch that.

So the judicial system isn't the answer, so what's left? What's left for people of color to do? Well it seems like the only thing left for us to do is accept our deaths because we can't do anything else. This makes me think of another interesting thing – America was willing to take Blacks as slaves but can't take in refugees. Yet, we are a country of immigrants, except for Native Americans, of course. It doesn't make any sense. Many people say, "We don't want these refugees in this country. They don't deserve to be over here." Okay then, so how many of you, by a show of hands, would love to trade places with a refugee? I'll wait...I didn't think so. You can't tell me that if America got as bad as other places, that you wouldn't do everything in your power to get your family to safety. You would do anything to ensure that you didn't have to worry about them on any given night and that all of their needs were being met. You tell me you wouldn't do that for your family? That's why most European immigrants came here, but now, it's not okay.

It saddens me still whenever I walk into a room I have to prove my intelligence. It's actually quite disheartening when I tell people that I have my master's degree and instead of them saying "Oh wow, that's great." they say something along the lines "You? You're so young!" Or when I'm talking to parents and students and they say, "I'd like to talk to an adult." That's always interesting as if my color defines or cancels out my age, experience, or professional training; or that my color defines my knowledge and abilities. Sometimes when I walk into a room with individuals I don't know, I smile. This is to ensure that everyone's not thrown off or that no one feels like I make them uncomfortable. I don't know if you've ever had to feel like that. What does it mean to be overly friendly for someone of color? It means to show that you're not a threat. It hurts sometimes because when it comes to issues dealing with people of color, I actually may have a say. Then again, maybe I might not. But you won't know until you add me as part of your *diverse* group.

Along the way I have learned that a lot of people who look like me aren't necessarily for me. There were times when I thought that it was only people who were not of color that were out to get me and that people of color were on my side. That's not always the case. There are people of color who want to see you drown as well. I can't tell you how many times I have talked to Black folks and they were just completely rude to me. People saying, "Oh you got a master's degree, who do you think you are?" and "Oh you're too good working up there at the university, huh?" If commenting on my dedication and success isn't enough, I hear "I see you traveling doing this and that." Haters are interesting individuals. It's honestly entertaining. There has to be something – some light, something special in your soul – that they are trying to squash. I want everybody to be successful. If you ask me how I did it, not only would I tell you how to do it, but I would also show you how to do it. At some point, for the haters, you have to actually appreciate them because they saw something so special inside you, something so great, that they were angry you had it and they didn't. There was something inside them telling them that they couldn't do what you were doing. Sometimes, I don't feel like the things I'm doing are really all that special. Sometimes I really feel like I'm just bells and whistles, but there has to be some innate gift that keeps you striving to do more and succeed beyond your initial goals or limitations.

Sometimes as a Black man, I'm afraid of losing my Black card – the membership to the Black community that you automatically get by just being Black. There are several ways you could lose this, like not watching the movie *Boyz n the Hood*, or not knowing how to do the Electric Slide. It wasn't until last year that I saw the movie *Friday*. Someone actually said "What the heck? You've never seen these movies, I'm white and I've seen these movies!" It just wasn't a thing that I was interested in. Having to still have one foot in the Black community and one foot out the Black community is a very hard position to navigate. You immediately know whether you're accepted or you're not accepted depending on what area you are currently standing in.

How is my Blackness truly defined? Is it defined by the way I walk? Is it defined by what pair of shoes I have on my feet or if I have any ice around my neck? Is my Blackness defined by the way that I speak? Is my Blackness best identified by how my face looks on particular day? I just think that a system that was never meant for us will never be able to help us. I think back to Emmett Till, a young Black man who was horrendously and horrifically killed for allegedly whistling at a white woman. Almost 40 years later, the woman who accused him admitted that she told a lie. Have you actually seen a picture of Emmett Till? If you haven't, go look him up. Did this punishment meet the crime? It's heartbreaking to know how he was killed, a true horror. He was shot, beaten,stabbed, and then he was dragged. He was mercilessly and viciously killed. For this woman to come out in 2017 and say it was a lie is absolutely disgusting. Then, she put it in a memoir and said the memoir won't be released for another five years. Where's the justice in that? So she's going to leave the legacy of a book that everyone is going to buy. Her family will profit from this book, but still this young man will never get justice? His mother had an open casket so everyone could see the horrific and brutal acts that were happening to men of color at that time. She wanted people to see that he was unrecognizable. People said that they could smell his body from one side of town to the other, but still there was no justice. None!

So where do we feel safe as Black people? Where's our safe space? Where is our area to go so that we don't have to go through the violence or the prejudice of racism? Is it in our own homes? Is it within our own families? Do we come out with Black owned businesses run by Black employees from Black CEOs? Do we funnel money into our own financial system? Some people think that that's the way that we should go. Some people think that we need to learn how to function within the areas in which we're given. Others think that we should be happy that we were brought over here, and now due to the Emancipation Proclamation, we're all free. We should be able to all go out there and make a living for ourselves and be able to make the best out of what we can get. My suggestion is that we need to all learn how to coexist. There are going to be people of color, people from different religions, sexual orientations, backgrounds, languages, socioeconomic statuses, educational levels, and abilities. We need to be able to figure out how we can all exist in this global marketplace and become global citizens.

What we do here in America definitely has an effect on what happens around the world. We don't need to feel isolated. We don't need to feel alone, even though at times we do. As a Black man I can tell you that there are times I absolutely feel isolated and alone, like nobody cares and no one wants you. Sometimes, it feels like everybody wants to see you fail and never to succeed. That anythingyou say has to be pulled apart just because of the color of your skin. All of this is because you just can't possibly be right. Then I thought, talking about us living as global citizens, what would happen if Blacks just remain silent and they didn't get involved? I think about what would happen if the Blacks were silent during the recent Muslim ban and only white people advocated for this group. What would happen? Or what if Blacks sat out on the Women's March on Washington? I think back on some of the larger issues in recent times – the crack epidemic, the constant criticism of Obama, and when men of color were being shot dead without cause. Where are all the advocates for us? Don't get me wrong, there were some non-Black advocates, but not many when you think that non-Blacks are over 80% of the population. White people have shown up but it seems like there are more that stay silent when these issues arise versus when it's something that directly affects them.

So yes, some Black people feel alone, they feel isolated, they feel forgotten, they feel that they put this country on their back and they were never rewarded or acknowledged. There were men of color that went overseas and fought for this country, but when they came back they still couldn't use the same bathroom as a white man. They couldn't sit down at the counter for a cup of coffee. Think about all the Black inventors, mathematicians, and scientists who progressed this country. Think about the cities that were built on the backs of slaves, but yet they are left out of history books. So please believe me when I say that these are the real fears of Black people.

It reminds of an experiment that scientists did with rats during the 1970s. They placed a family of rats in a small box. The family consisted of a father, a mother, and two babies. As long as the family was fed and given proper water, the rats were fine in their small box. The moment the scientists limited their water and took away their food, you saw the father rat turn on the babies and eventually ate them. What can you expect when resources are low and survival is an absolute necessity? You can clearly see the breakdown of the rat family. It's the same thing that happens in the "hood." If you take away the male parent, assuming that it is a heterosexual two-parent family unit, that family unit can break down just like the rats did. Thinking back to judicial system for Black men, this is all too common. Did I mention you need to watch *13th* on Netflix?

Now Black folk, don't get me wrong, we have much work to do on our end as well. Many of our communities are broken. The crime rates in our communities have risen. We sometimes cannot unify or come together when it's most important. We allow loud and arrogant people to speak out for our communities instead of showing up. Lastly, over the course of generations, Black men have allowed a breakdown in the

87

family structure. Yes, I said allowed. For me to sit here and provide insight as to the challenges that we face, we must first take a look at ourselves. No one is going to help our community, this is strictly up to us. We have to continue to invest in our younger Black generations. They are the future. We need to invest in math, sciences, politics, and Black enterprise. In our inner cities, why are parents more concerned about what's on our children's feet rather than what's in their heads?

Whenever we talk about famous and influential Black people in the community, we always go back to the greats. Frederick Douglass, Thurgood Marshall, Harriet Tubman, Rosa Parks, Martin Luther King Jr., George Washington Carver, Malcom X, Huey P. Newton, Barack Obama, and so on. Is this all that we have? What other influential leaders do our Black students have to look up too? These names always come up. We need more influential leaders for our youth to look up to in 2017. What about, Valerie Jarrett, John Conyers, Jr., Mellody Hobson, Cheryl Boone, Toni Morrison, Neil deGrasse Tyson, Maxine Waters, John Lewis, Marian Wright Edelman, Van Jones, and Cornel West? Do you know who all of these famous and influential Black leaders? I don't expect you to. They are not highlighted in our community. We always want to praise the ghost of our people, not that they shouldn't be recognized for all that they have done. But when do we move on to say there are Black individuals who are now taking the helm and moving us forward? We should be pushing our students to be the next Jesse Williams, Leslie Odom Jr., Charlene Carruthers, Ava DuVernay, Chadwick Boseman, Sage Steele, Issa Rae, and Misty Copeland. If you don't know these names, I guess you have some homework to do.

My biggest fear is that one day, the Black voice will be forgotten and we will become a permanent underclass. We'll never be able to rise up and truly become the people that we need to be. It's just a small fear, but fears aren't necessarily reality. The reality is that everyone, including those who want to wish bad fortune onto others, will always rise up to something better. No one can do it alone. I don't want to imagine a society where Blacks just sit stuff out. We can't sit out! We participated too much to simply give up on this country. We still go to war, we still show up at the marches, campaign rallies, and protests. We still show up at the voting booth knowing that it might not even turn out in our favor. Why? The answer is because we cannot do it all alone. We, as a people, don't want to continue to carry America on our backs. We want everybody to equally share the load with us. That's what we need to move forward. That is what we need to stop our people from being wrongly killed and incarcerated. That is why Black Lives Matter.

Chapter 7
Cultural Differences

Throughout my life and time working with diversity programs, I've seen a lot of cultural differences. Working with admissions for about five years has really shown me some interesting things when it comes to enrollment. Firstly, let's talk about the marketing because it's honestly funny sometimes. Whenever they send out pamphlets or booklets to prospective students, the institution makes sure to include something relatable to everyone. For our students who want to be scientist, they'll see a picture of a student in their white coat working in a lab. The student athletes see people scoring that winning point or making that amazing play. But then you turn to the page about diversity, and that is one of the funniest! You're going to see students who are Black, Asian, Latinx, and white. Maybe you'll even someone in a wheelchair, someone wearing a LGBTQIA pride shirt, or maybe someone in Greek letters. This big group is going to be sitting together in the dining hall or hanging out on the quad. Theylook like all-inclusive best friends inviting you to come hang out with them. Talk about modern day *Breakfast Club*, huh? Unfortunately, that's not how our college campuses look. To start out with, is that even an accurate representation of the population? More likely than not, that one picture shows an extremely skewed representation of the campus demographic. Overall, however, it doesn't look like this picture because college is what you make of it. Unfortunately, a lot people stick to people who are similar to themselves. That's why on college campuses you still see the athletes over here, Greek life over there, groups of white students here, groups of Black students over there.

When we're talking about cultural diversity, we're also talking about the qualities of those individual cultures. We're looking at their beliefs, opinions, customs, food, clothes, and religions. So, when I'm thinking about cultural differences, I'm thinking about all these things. I know throughout this book we've already talked a lot about white and Black issues, but I have another example about the cultural difference, so bear with me. Sometimes when I'm facilitating a workshop, I ask the audience, "If you're a person of color do not respond." I then say, "If you're a white person, or if you identify as being white, please sing me happy birthday." Everybody sings the somewhat monotone version of the song. Then I say, if you're Black, sing me happy birthday and everybody laughs and sings "Happy birthday to ya, Happy birthday to ya, happy birthdayyyy!" and everyone jumps up and starts dancing. Every person who's white in the audience gets this really funny look on their face like, "What the heck is going on, like what is this new song?" They start leaning over to their Black friends asking, "When did you learn this?" Then I make a joke, like, "Well before the presentation, me and all the Black students got together and we rehearsed this number."

Some cultural tendencies cannot be explained, yet they are so funny. For example, I have concluded that white people and Black people play the game UNO differently. I promise you. When I speak with white people, they play by the official rules given inside the box. However, when I play with Black folk, they all have different versions of the way they play. It's ridiculous. Has anyone ever heard of the word "stacksies?" Of course you have, so why do you and everyone play the game so differently? Even how different cultures see food is differently. I know that if I have you over my house, we are going to have a spread. This includes a meat, vegetable, starch, and dessert. Yet, when I went over some of my best friend's house for dinner, they would try and feed me cheese, crackers, a vegetable and fruit platter and say we ate dinner.

It's interesting because we all start laughing and it gets everyone energized and comfortable. Then we start talking about other kinds of cultural difference we have. One of the big ones that I always point out is how individuals say hello. I often refer back to this one story where a colleague and I were walking down the street and I happened to see another Black man

91

walking towards me. As we got closer to each other, the Black guy dapped me up – no pun intended on Diversity Awareness Program. He gave me a little handshake and said "Hey, how you doing?" and I responded "Good, you?" He said, "Good." and we walked our separate ways. My colleague, who happened to be white, looks at me puzzled and says, "So, who was that?" And I said, "I don't know...some Black dude." My colleague was confused and said "Well, you said 'Hi' to him, didn't you?" I responded "Well yeah, that's just what we do. Black people say what's up to each other." He didn't believe me that Black people just say 'hi" to each other in passing. He said, "Justin, if this is one of your diversity games, I'm not in the mood for it today." I assured him this wasn't a game by saying "No, it's a cultural difference. It's not something that's good or bad, it's just something that Black people do when we see each other; we say 'hi' to each other." He said, "Well I'm white I don't say 'hi' to every single white person that I see." I laughed and said "Yeah, I know, because literally you would just line everybody up, and handshake people or high-five everybody as you're walking down the street." He still didn't believe me, but he saw a Black guy walking across the street and told me to go say 'hi' to him. I said, "It doesn't work that way. There are levels to this. Every single Black guy I see, I don't walk up to him and say 'Hello fellow Black man.' It doesn't work like that. Chances are, if he makes eye contact with me, we'll probably connect and we'll probably speak to each other." To prove my point, I tried to draw attention to me so this guy across the street would make eye contact with me. When the Black guy across the street and I connected, he gave me the head nod. It looked like my white colleague mind just exploded. He said, "I just didn't know that these things existed."

So readers, I want to know how many cultural experiences you are having. Are you taking time to really get to know aspects about other people's culture? Are you really taking the time to have those instructive and informative experiences? I ask, because I know of many different features that cultural difference play into. For example, in the United States, we take a lot of time to make sure we tip our servers in a restaurant. But, I know in Japan and South Korea, tipping is seen as an insult. However, in America, it's common practice and expected. When we're happy in America we give thumbs up, meaning approval, agreement, or encouragement. In the Middle East and in Latin America the thumb up doesn't have the same meaning. It's almost like giving the middle finger and nobody likes being given the middle finger. In America, when you're out with your friends at a bar and someone has fancy drink or the specialty beer it's fairly common to share a taste. But, did you know in Norway is considered extremely rude and distasteful? It's all about getting to take the time to truly get to know others and understand their cultures.

Let's bring some of the stuff we talked about in the chapter on perception here. As we know, perception is the lens with which we view the world. This also comes into play when we talk about cultural diversity because there are perceived characteristics of other cultures. Some of these are harmful stereotypes. Sometimes, I think there's a double standard when it comes to the way that people of color are perceived versus white people. This is something that we place on each other in the community, and how others outside the community view us. For instance, as a 27yearold Black man, let's say I had eighteen kids. What would my reputation be on the streets? Well it probably wouldn't be good. People would probably say I was a player, that I was irresponsible, or just someone's baby daddy. Yet if you're white and have nineteen kids, you get a show on TLC called *Nineteen Kids and Counting*. Also, what if I had multiple wives or girlfriends, maybe even had kids with all of them? What would people probably say about me? They would probably say that I was a player, a pimp, or someone who didn't really value women. But again, if you are white, you get a TV show on TLC called *Sister Wives*. As a network, TLC clearly shows white privilege and cultural perceptions. But it's not just TLC– Lifetime currently has a show called *Married at First Sight*. So, in America, we get entertainment out of two strangers meeting once and getting married. Yet, we ridicule other cultures that value arranged marriages.

How do you go about managing cultural differences? The first step is realizing you are not an expert – I never consider myself an expert and I work in this field. There is always more to learn and room to grow. Even as a diversity trainer, I'm constantly learning, reshaping, and redefining my definitions of diversity, multiculturalism, and cultural awareness. There are new things that I'm learning every day. Sometimes, I think the sessions are more beneficial for me as the facilitator versus when I was a participant. I have learned so much through the course of ten years. I have encountered over half a million people, each with unique stories, backgrounds, beliefs, ideas, and innovative ways to bring people together. I do not believe that the country is split, although, in reality, it may be. I think that if you actually take the time to individually speak to each person, we all have the same roles. We all have the same wants. We all have the same desires. Everybody wants the ability to have food. Everyone wants to be loved. Everybody wants to have a say. Everyone wants to be heard. People want to know that they have a heart. I do not innately think that everyone in this world is evil. I think there are good people in this world, but sometimes they're just clouded by those who are not as good or didn't make the best choices. I think there are people in this world who really want to do right by people, really truly want to understand how the world operates, and want to make a difference.

One of the most important things we can leave behind is our knowledge; what we have learned through life that we can share with others. One of the biggest parts of this is being a globally minded person. This is a person who can see the cultural difference and find values in others ways of life and their beliefs. That leaves the biggest question – can you actually spot cultural differences? Would you know a cultural difference if you saw one? I mean there are a lot of different common concepts or themes when it comes to cultural differences; body language, manners, religious beliefs or practices, reactions to problems, mealtimes, greetings, hygiene, family structure, perception of time, gender roles. All those things have to do with cultural differences. Would you even know them if you saw them? I know all of those things sound different but I also know that we all smile in the same language.

We need to realize that cultural knowledge in the workplace is necessary. Meaning, how colleagues represent and share their culture in the workplace and navigate that space based on their experience. Keep in mind that cultures change over time – they are influenced by economic advancement, globalization, technology, new beliefs, and the influences of other cultures. And of course, these differences in culture influence how people conduct themselves through life, including at work. Can you make room for cultural differences in your life? Think about it. As a reader, are you really willing to bend what you believe and be flexible? So that you can live your everyday life,and so that other individuals can be able to live theirs too? I often think of a colleague of mine who was from another country– I honestly can't recall from which country. Whenever this colleague decides to talk to me, he speaks very, very closely. Even when I take a step back he takes a step forward. He's literally in my face as if he's about to whisper something to me, but he is at a normal conversational level. Even though it is very uncomfortable for me, I respect that this is how they communicate in his culture. They don't have the same customary proximity rules as we do in America. You know, the leave the empty seat between you and that stranger system or shuffling to the far corners of the elevator so you don't bump shoulders. As with any person learning and adjusting to a different culture, he forgets sometimes. I try to remind him that he's a bit too close and that people may be turned off by that proximity. And guess what? I don't think he does that out of malice or trying to be intentionally invasive in my private space. But I also don't just blame him either. I have to become flexible knowing that he is more comfortable being closer, so I meet him in the middle. This shows that I value his cultural preference, but also mine is valued as well.

It's all about managing cultural differences. You have to be able to manage and be flexible at the same time. You also have to be aware of how cultural differences affect our day-to-day lives. These differences have a significant impact on how our nation seeks to understand others and learn different viewpoints. Let's look back to how the media describes different cultures. For example, a certain someone that I know said that all Mexicans are rapists. I don't believe that. To find out for myself, I went down to Mexico in winter 2016. I had a wonderful time in Cancun and at the ruins of Chichen Itza. I got to jump into the Cenote. I went to Isla Mujeres and I had the best time of my life! But the whole time I was over there I was just really fascinated with how rich, prosperous, and very accommodating their culture was. And when I say rich, I don't mean monetarily, I mean by beliefs, hospitality, how they treat foreigners, how kind people were, the culture, the music, and the food. It was prevalent and I felt immersed in their culture. I didn't feel like I was American – just for a second, it felt like I was one of them because of how welcoming they were. In fact, I felt more welcomed over there than I ever have been in America. Oftentimes, I think about all the messages that the media says about people who are Mexican. How dangerous they are. People who say that Mexicans are taking their jobs, but has it happened to them personally? Have you seen a Mexican personally take your job? If not, that's not necessarily something you should say. Do you know of anybody where a Mexican has taken his or her job? Think about the 10 closest people to you in your life, did Mexicans take their jobs? Probably not. Yet, that's always the tagline when we talk about immigration. Mexicans in this country are working jobs that people don't want to work. Most times when you see Mexicans, they aren't CEOs of companies, or creating policy in our government, they're doing the hard, backbreaking work that most Americans wouldn't do. So again, how are they stealing our jobs?

Some people also state how Mexicans are a threat to our democracy and freedom. Well, I got a taste of how threatening a Mexican was while I was visiting their beautiful country. After a night out, I came across a fouryearold boy named Manuel. It was about 4:00am. Manuel came up to me with the saddest face of any child I've have ever seen in my life. He was up at this early hour selling bracelets. I sat down with Manuel for a little bit and we actually talked using my very limited amount of Spanish that I learned back in high school. After talking with Manuel, I was able to figure out that he was selling these bracelets so that he could provide for his family. So, of course I bought a few bracelets, but I also broke bread with Manuel and tried to learn more about his life. Of course, this wasn't the easiest with my limited Spanish, but one of the best things I got from it was when he said "Me gusto Star Wars." or "I like Star Wars." It really made me think about the about the political comments that are happening in our country. I looked right into Manuel's eyes and I thought, "This is the person that's a threat to me?" These are the dangerous individuals that we're looking for? This little boy who likes Star Wars and is trying to make things better for his family? It really gave me an opportunity to sit back and think of how many things we're programmed to think. How we are susceptible to accepting what we're told or what the media pushed on us. I ended up taking some pictures with him. He really liked that. To think that if a giant wall was actually placed between Manuel and me, we would have never had this experience.

The next day when I was walking through town, I saw Manuel again, this time with his father. His father looked exhausted from working all day. Manuel came up and gave me a high-five. I looked at his father and I said "Hola." and he responded with "Hello...you're American, right?" And I said, "Yeah, yeah, I'm American." He said, "Okay, cool, I speak English." And I thought wait a minute, in my mind I just thought that everybody that I was coming in contact with only spoke Spanish. I asked him where you learnedEnglish. He said, "I'm an American; I just live in Mexico with my family. I was born in America but after I lived there for a while, I came back to Mexico." He asked how I met Manuel and I told him that we met last night and I bought some bracelets. He said "Yeah, things are really, really hard down here and I just really want the best for him and I want the best for our family. I don't make a lot of money but we got family right?" I nodded. Even though he looked like he'd been working so hard that day, he still had a smile on his face. It looked like he been through every single hardship that you can think have but he seemed happy. Manuel was up at 4:00am, yet he was happy. There's just something about that experience that I wouldn't trade for the world. These people don't seem like bad people or people that want to do us harm as Americans. They just seems like people who want to live a good life and want to have great experiences as well, there's nothing wrong with that.

We talk about how different each person is because of their experiences and their cultures. We talk about how they were raised, their religion, the socioeconomic status, how and where they were educated, their family, and their friends. We can see how people can be so different compared to the person standing next to them. We have to remember that saying "all white people" or "all Black people" isn't accurate – people conduct themselves differently. When we talk about these concepts, it's very interesting to see where they come from in regards to their culture. At a workshop, I played this game called *Ask Any Race Whatever Question You Want.* It's a very interesting game because you could only imagine the type of questions that people ask. Some of the questions consist of people of color asking white people "Is clapping on beat really that difficult?" Some white people have responded by saying, "I just cannot get it, I can't get it; it's the same reason why I can't dance." then ask back "How do Black people dance so well?" Black people explain "It's just rhythm, you don't have rhythm?" Some just say white people don't have rhythm, and some white people agree with that. But then some white people disagree with "Oh my gosh no, I have rhythm, that's not a thing. Look!" then they proceed to get up and dance. A white person asked a Black person, "What's the big difference in our hair? There's not really a big difference is there?" And the Black person responded by saying, "Oh yes there is. There is a huge difference!" They went on to explain the significance of the hair and ended with "And can I touch it?" Nope, you cannot, so don't ask." Everyone in the audience laughed.

98

Someone brought up a question about depression, so we talked about mental illness as it is something many people face. From my experiences, when white people talk about mental illness, they talk about resources and medication – they accept that this is something that exists. Where people in the Black community – again, from my experience – don't really refer to mental illness or accept it as a real thing. They might say, "You just need to take some time off."or "You're trippin'." You hear, "You need to go to church, you need to pray it away." I wish my culture paid more attention to mental illness because it's something that is real and affects our community. The issue of mental illness recently came to light when a rap artist named Kid Cudi checked himself into a mental institution. I think that is when young Black men really started seeing mental illness as a real thing. Other Black celebrities have brought to light the damaging effects of mental illness if not treated as well. While more light is being shined in this area, I'm still afraid mental illness isn't recognized in the Black community.

I remember in one of my sessions, someone from the Black community wanted to know if white people actually had family reunions or was that just a Black thing. They responded by saying, "Absolutely we have family reunions. We might not have them every year but family reunions are like our equivalent to Thanksgiving." People from the Black community said that they are used to having barbeques and get-togethers all year long. Black people asked white people why some whites riot when they win sports games,but also when they lose games. The white people responded by saying, "It's just fun to riot. But I don't necessarily think that's true for everybody." As the facilitator doing these activities as a focus group,I know these comments aren't necessarily a true thing, nor should they be taken as facts. Just like when people say, "Racism is over because the president was Black." Well, you know that simply isn't true. Diversity doesn't equal white genocide. It doesn't mean that minorities will one day take over the world and we'll all be so mixed that white people will die out. What it means is that we're all becoming a blended nation. There won't be a Blacks or white only section in Heaven, so we may as well all start to get to know each other and get along now.

One funny question that was asked by someone from the white community to people of color was, "How come Black people are always screaming in movie theaters during horror movies?" Everyone laughed. People from the Black community responded by saying, "Well we're screaming because white people are always making the dumb mistakes and they're getting killed...we're trying to save you all. 'Hurry up, get out of there.' Ya'll don't really listen." As a facilitator, my observations of this game are that individuals truly let their guards down. They become fully immersed in the dialogue and truly ask some serious questions. Again, there are many questions that are asked that are simply silly, but you get a sense that the separated group starts to blend. It's no longer an "us versus them" mentality.

The questions continue to go back and forth. I remember once, someone from the white community asked, "Why are you Black people so offended when people use the 'N' word but you use it all the time?" It was interesting to see the responses on this question because the Black audience was split on this particular subject. Some of the Black participants responded by saying, "I don't like the 'N' word either. It's terrible and should never be used." Some other Blacks tried to justify it saying, "We use the 'N' word as a term of endearment. We don't mean it in the negative connotation." Language and reclaiming words is an interesting thing. What does the 'N' word mean now? And, who has the right and privilege over the 'N' word? Who has the ability to say when it's appropriate and who is allowed say it?

There were many important questions brought up, and we can't go into every single one, but I like to point out the questions that caused a lot of discussion. One of those questions was the debate on whether Jesus was a person of color. In modern America, he's always depicted as being someone who is light skinned with long, wavy hair, strong muscles, and blue eyes. The bible teaches that Jesus was from the Middle East. It says his hair was like wool and his skin was like bronze. These characteristics mean that he was probably a man of color. Many

100

different questions stemmed from that original question. I think one of my favorite questions was, "How come Black people seem to have ghetto names?" There were some interesting responses and comments at this question. It seemed the conclusion on that question was that Black parents want to make their children have special or unique names. There are some parents that go as far as to name their child Uniqua. My mom did the very same thing. Who has a middle name like LaKyle? That's not a thing but everybody wants their child to have a unique name. I bet you there's no other Justin LaKyle Brown in this world other than me. My conclusion with this activity is that we have to continue to bring people together. Whether that's by hosting programs, having developmental conversations, or by having programs with learning outcomes that support the initiatives of our institutions.

Again, I must point out that during this activity, it is usually people who are white and people who are Black that are very active. Not many questions are asked of other races or backgrounds, in fact, many people from different races or backgrounds often remain silent or untouched. Why do you think that is? In my opinion, I believe it's because, again, in America, we only care about and focus on issues of Black or white. Things cannot be like that. They are not this or that. There has to be some gray area. I'd be interested in pointing this out in the future to gain reasoning as to why those individuals do not speak up or ask more questions. My observations show me that they are merely continuing to learn the culture. They do so by observing the activity, rather than participating.

In conclusion, this chapter brings me to a very funny story that my grandfather always told whenever he went to multicultural churches. It's a funny story that I'm actually stealing but giving him the credit. My grandfather often tells this story about a zebra that died and went to heaven. It wanted to know, once and for all, the answer to an age-old question. Was he a zebra that was black with white stripes or a zebra that was white with black stripes? So he went to go ask John the Baptist and said, "Hey, I want to finally answer the age old question."

John the Baptist said, "What's that?" The zebra asked, "Am I a white zebra with black stripes or a black zebra with white stripes?" John the Baptist said, "Well, hold on I'll go ask the maker (God)." Later on he came back and said to the zebra, "Zebra, I have an answer for you." The zebra said, "What is it?" John the Baptist said, "You are what you are." The zebra said, "Oh that makes perfect sense. That means that I'm a white zebra with black stripes." John the Baptist was confused and asked "How do you figure that?" The zebra then stated, "Because, if the maker had told me I was a black zebra with white stripes, he would have said, 'You is what you is.'" I tell that joke often and audiences always meet me with laughter. A very funny joke, but nevertheless, it brings people together and makes a point. Different cultures work so much more effectively when we can work together collaboratively rather than being at odds with one another.

Chapter 8
Battle of the Genders

Anything you can do, I can do better. I can do anything better than you. No you can't – yes I can! No you can't – yes I can! One of the most famous battles of all time is this battle between men and women. Who's better, who's more equipped, who's the smartest, and who should be running the country? Is a certain gender more athletic than the other? Should they get paid more than the other? These age-oldbattles are happening every day. As a society we have yet to figure out if there are even answers to these questions. I personally think there should be gender equality in all aspects of life, so I think the answer is neither. It shouldn't matter what your gender is or how you identify. Everyone should receive equal treatment. Unfortunately, our society doesn't work like that. Gender inequality is a real thing. It refers to the unequal treatment of individuals based on their gender, generally women. This inequality is evident in regards to opportunities, salary, experiences, and overall treatment. This happens to women much more than it does for men in regards to their careers, education, economic advancement, or political influence. There are several different gender based activities that we play and I want to talk about those in this chapter, as well as the differences that I've learned between men and women.

Before moving forward, we need to discuss gender and gender identity. Even though a lot of this chapter focuses on men and women, as a society we need to recognize that gender is beyond a binary. Not every person is cisgender, meaning they are female/feminine and identifies as a woman, or male/masculine and identifies as a man. Just as there are many ways for individuals to identify their sexuality, there are many forms of gender identity. Let's not forget about our Trans and genderqueer communities who certainly face many inequalities in our society. As a cisgender man, I have a privilege I must recognize – it's easy for me to automatically talk about issues that directly affect me. I want you to know that when it comes to this chapter, I writing from my perspective. Yes, as someone who works in the diversity education field, I try to check my privilege, but I'm not perfect. I wanted to let you know that this chapter may appear very biased when it comes that view, but I didn't want you to think that I had forgotten about you all. You play an intricate part in our society and it needs to be recognized.

Being transgender can mean many things and can be represented in many different ways – after all, it is about how that person identities. Generally speaking, a Trans person is someone whose sense of personal identity and gender does not correspond with the sex and gender automatically assigned at birth. This means that a person's outward representation may not align with their internal self. There are so many ways this is represented in a person, but many automatically think of a man who sees themself as a woman and therefore presents as a woman, or vice versa. This is not all that Trans is – each person is in a different stage of understanding of who they are and each presents and identifies that self in different ways. Before the chapter truly begins, I want to ensure that you know what it means to be Trans, at least from my understanding, considering I am self-aware and recognize that I am not Trans and cannot truly speak on those issues. It's important that individuals stay informed and become allies. Attend an ally training. That training is priceless and a great start. How can you be an ally of transgender individuals? Well first, you can't tell that someone is transgender just by looking at them. Transgender people don't have a "look." We can't make assumptions about others. If you're not sure of what pronouns to use, you need to ask because defining someone else's pronouns is inappropriate and disrespectful. I remember when Caitlyn Jenner transitioned into a woman and identified by she/her/hers. People would say, "No, no, no, no, Bruce Jenner is still a man and I'm going to identify him as a man." Well, that decision is not up to you. It's up to the individual and how they want to be identified and we have to support and respect that.

In the same way that it is impolite to assume someone's

pronouns, it's also rude to ask transgender individuals what their real name is. Their name is exactly what they choose it to be. We have to be open and accepting of who that individual is and not dwell on what society assigned to them at birth. In the same regards, we have to be respectful – just because a Trans person has come out to you, it doesn't mean they are out to the world. I recall doing training for individuals who were all males and based on the discussions, I assume the majority of the rooms werecisgender and heterosexual. The group said "Justin, I can't mess with these transgender people. They make me confused, they freak me out, and I just don't get it." I replied back, "Well, what freaks you out when you're talking about individuals who identify as transgender?" The student stated, "What freaks me out is I don't know if I'm talking to a man or a woman. I could be standing there talking to a woman that has a penis. I don't know if the woman has a penis or not so I got to ask." I was a bit confused, so I asked, "So that is your relationship advice to men who are trying to talk to women. You go up to every single woman and say, 'Hey I noticed you looking at me and I want to know do you have a penis?'" Everyone in the audience died of laughter.

This is not the way you would approach anyone you were trying to romantically pursue, or communicate with in general. Knowing what sexual organ a person has does not change how you talk to them and not knowing shouldn't make you uncomfortable. So, going up and asking people that question is not okay, it's none of your concern unless that person wants to share this identity with you. I'm not from the transgender community, so I can't speak upon their issues, what they feel, or how they're being discriminated against. I can become an ally. I want to use the opportunity to speak upon these issues to show that I am an ally and encourage you to become an ally too. Becoming an ally is more than just words. It's a call to action. If you are not actively doing something, you are not an ally. Having a sticker on your door claiming your office as a Safe Space isn't enough. You have to stay up to date on issues and be part of the movement.

Respecting the terminology is important for all people, especially those in the LGBTQIA community. You must be cognizant of your language and be respectful of those transitioning or questioning. It's not for you to decide who someone else is. Some of the most alarming things I hear is that people purposefully calling a Trans person out of name or saying "Well, they have to be gay. Look at them." and "Bi isn't real. Just pick a side. You're confused." My friends in the LGBTQIA community often tell me that there is a lot of discrimination amongst them. People not accepting Trans people, bisexuals, queer, questioning, and so forth within their own community. This occurs by other LGBTQIA people promoting the misconception that bisexual can't be monogamous or are confused. It is gay men shaming each other for body type and appearance. You see it with lesbians claiming true lesbians are those who hold the "gold star," meaning those who had never been with a man. But again, I am not a member of this community, so I can't speak on its behalf. I am just sharing stories I hear from friends or throughout my work each day. Either way, we all, regardless of how you identify, need to stop putting others down just so we can feel better. We have got to be better.

We've got to make sure that we have trans-inclusive communities. I think that that's really important topic. Is your language, friends, or the company that you keep trans-inclusive? If you had a friend who identified as Trans, would you be comfortable bringing them into your community? Do we take time to listen to transgender individual's needs and wants? We need to support gender-neutral bathrooms. I don't know why Target had such a big backlash. At the end of the day, everybody has to go to the bathroom. Who cares which door they go into? Are we truly listening or are we saying, "I have a Trans friend so that means that I'm Trans-friendly?" Again, that's not *being* an ally. Being and ally is a call to action; having the ability to support those individuals in the ways that they need to be supported not what we think is best for them. And, at the end of the day, like I said, I'm not from the Trans community.

Therefore, I know my limits as should you as the reader. You're not going to be able to do everything. Sometimes being an ally means showing up and shutting up. I learned this concept when I went to my first *Speak Out*. This was an enlightening opportunity to hear the testimonies and heartbreaking stories of individuals. It truly changed my life because I didn't see what life without my privilege could be like. Sometimes, we need to just be a physical presence. This is sometimes the best support we can offer. Just because you are not speaking doesn't mean you are not effective. Those are my tips for working with people who may identify differently than you. Again, I want to reiterate that this chapter is really going to focus on my experiences dealing with men and women that mostly identify as cisgender and heterosexual. I wanted to make sure that I did not leave anybody out of the conversation and that this book was inclusive for all readers.

Getting back to the chapter, growing up as a Black male, I was taught many different things, especially when it comes to women. I was taught you don't hit girls. I was taught you hold the door open for women and always remain chivalrous. I was taught to use manners, don't curse around women, and make sure they're okay. I was taught to make sure that they're on the inside of the sidewalk when you're walking down the street. If they're cold you give them your jacket and if it's raining hold the umbrella open for them. When you're out and about, make sure that you protect them. I always ask students whether or not they think chivalry is dead. Most of my male students will say, "Yeah, chivalry is dead and it was killed by women." This is a question I really want to examine. Is chivalry really dead? Are these concepts that I just talked about, which I adapted from the way my father raised me, still concepts that people follow today, or does it not matter? Gender equality is important. It should not matter whether you are a male or female; everyone should be treated equally. As a male growing up, I found that there were times that I did things chivalrously, but they not received so well. For example, I would hold doors for ladies and they would tell me that they could open the door themselves. If I tried to

107

help a young lady who was trying to pick up a heavy box, and I was told she could do it herself. I started to realize that, maybe what I was taught isn't applicable in the world today or appreciated by modern women. I have met several females who still appreciate a chivalrous man and look for that quality. Do women want men to be chivalrous but still respect that they are their own independent individuals? What does that look like?

Now we'll go back to the original topic of the chapter, the battle of the genders. There are two activities on this topic. The first game is very similar to *This or That*, except one side of the room is *Male* and the other side is *Female*. In this game called *This or That: Men and Women Edition*, I have a list of adjectivesthat do not pertain to any particular sex or gender at all. I begin to call out the words and ask the participants to choose what side they believe the word describes. But again, they cannot stand in the middle. There is no right or wrong answer. It's quite thought provoking to see how people determine why they chose either side.

So, let's take a look. I explain the rules to the group and everyone immediately gets excited! The first word is *Breadwinner*. The group splits up, some going to the men side, some to the women's side. I immediately go to the men's side, which is now a mix of men and women, just to see what they have to say. I hear things like, "My father brought home most of the bacon. He was our provider growing up." Then I go to the women's side. Many of those comments consists of how their parents are divorced, that their father wasn't active in their lives, or their father just split one day. They talked about the impact their mom made as a single parent; a mother raising them alone and providing for them. These individuals were saying their mother had multiple jobs, was going to school, and was still an active mother. When we talk about this *Breadwinner* concept, we really have to understand that the divorce rate is very high in America. Many people come from broken homes and single parent homes; this topic is really expressed in this session. They want to share because their experiences were different from those who had two parent homes or those with active fathers.

The participants go very deep in regards to their family history and experiences. Families aren't the little nuclear units of the past anymore where mom stays home taking care of the house and family while dad goes to work. Sure, this family structures still exists, but it is not the norm as it was 60 years ago. This story that describes dad coming home from a long day, right in time for dinner is no longer the American story. Lots of American families are being raised by one parent or a guardian. Children are not always being raised by a mom and dad – let's not forget about our same-sex parents either. We can't ignore all those dads who are single parents either. We so often talk about absent fathers, but sometimes moms split too. I hear countless stories of individuals who were raised by grandparents, aunts, uncles, teachers, coaches, and even church members. According to today's statistics, one third of American families are split up. It's not necessarily mom and dad anymore and this is a huge eye-opener for some students who've grown up with two happily married parents. It's unusual for them to hear about families having issues or families being separated by divorce. For some students, these are new concepts because it has not been their experience.

The next word I use is *Submissive*. Again, much like the first word, the students will choose whatever side they feel is right for them. The submissive one is very stimulating because depending on what type of attitude the particular male or female has will define their answer. Each word is purposefully ambiguous. This leaves the term up for interpretation by the participant. For example, when I go to the *Female* side, a lot of the women say, "Well, women are supposed to be submissive to their man; that's what the Bible says." or "I remember my mother being very submissive to my father." And then there are some on the *Female* side that say, "I would never submit to a man. My examples of men have not been that great; whether in relationships with men that I've been in or otherwise." Remember, you have to pick a side. There is no gray area. So, while this person would never be submissive, they still had to choose a side. It may not be their reality but they see the societal influence. Some students go into great detail about relationships with men where there was physical or emotional violence and bullying. A great deal of women, as well as men, felt forced into a submissive role by men in their lives. A lot of women go into great detail about their relationships with men or the examples that were or were not set by their fathers. Of course, violence does not just affect women, it affects men as well, and women can perpetuate violence too. This highlights their stance on why they will not be submissive. For the most part, the men standing on the *Female* side believe that women should be submissive or that is what society perpetrates, hence explaining where they stood.

The next word that I use in the activity is *Privilege*. *Privilege* is another thought-provoking term because the majority of people will go over to the *Male* side while there are only a few that stay on *Female* side. I always let the underdog go first so I go to the *Female* side where just a few women are standing. The women say, "We're privileged because we have more education. There are more women in college then there has ever been. There are smarter women. There are more women coming into science and technology." or "Women will always be privileged because we carry life." It's very fascinating when individuals talk about women carrying life. Where would men be without women? I think it's important to add that life does come from women, but that is not their sole purpose in life. So where do men get off saying what women should or should not be doing with their bodies? They attempt to make decision on whether or not they should be able to prevent pregnancy or have an abortion. It's remarkable that the government can also determine or dictate what women should do with their bodies. I digress – this *Privilege* term is very open ended and usually leads to the group talking about having children. Several women that are on the privilege side say, "I have the privilege to decide whether or not I want kids and it doesn't make me a bad person because I don't want them."

Normally, on the other side, people say that men have the privilege. Men make the world go round. Men are the

110

entrepreneurs. They're the ones that determine the rules that make up this country. Even though Beyoncé sings "Who run the world...girls," in retrospect, who really runs the world? The answer is the cisgender, heterosexual, Christian, white males. And once they get in government, they're the ones that make, execute, and enforce laws. They have the most money. They're the ones that develop policy. They're the ones that are usually in law enforcement. So when it comes to privilege, quite naturally, men are seen as those holding the privilege. But, does it apply to all men? What about men of color? What about LGBTQIA identified men? Does the same privilege apply to them, or are they just left out on the side? Are there different levels of privilege? So, as a man, can I be on the top tier of privilege, but then move down a notch for being Black, but still higher on the privilege scale than a woman? It's really exciting to knock out those concepts.

The next word that we use in this activity is *Nurturer*. Now, nurture is intriguing because it can be hit or miss; it just depends on who played the dominant role in an individual's life. Some males say they felt that their mothers were the nurturers, while some women felt their fathers were the nurturers. Interestingly enough, many people have problems with this one because the nurturer isn't always a parent. Sometimes a nurturer is a pastor, Sunday school teacher, coach, or a teacher. Sometimes a nurturer is a grandparent. Sometimes a nurturer is a very close neighbor or family friend. Nurturers aren't necessarily always family.

The words and terms continue to fly as we move along this activity. Some of the words used are *Smart, Intelligent, Violent,* and *Accommodating.* These words get students to break out of their shells and really try to hone in on what are the bigger issues. It is clear that the issues surrounding gender truly program us to believe we have specific roles in society. But, who determines gender roles? Are these determined straight from birth? Are these things that we learned in grade school? Are they just general concepts that are just picked up from society? How do we determine what is true or accurate in order to complete our roles?

People learn a lot about relationships based on what they observed growing up. For me, I think that relationships must be a 50-50 job. I know that in order to pick up a box, an individual needs two hands. Without two hands, you can't pick up the box. That's a 50-50 role even if one of the individuals in that role might be more dominant. For me, I'm right handed. So my right hand is dominant but there are a lot of things that my right hand can't do without my left hand. It's a 50-50-partnership making things work cohesively. Individuals need to work better at building relationships. In today's society, people just get up and run when things get hard. No one wants to tough it out because the focus is on me, me, ME!

In the sessions however, relationships are a central theme, especially breakups. After all, our experiences shape how we see the world. Breakups are rough! Have you ever been through a breakup? Have you ever had your heart broken? Have you had someone mislead you about who they were or what their intentions were? Have you had someone lie to you – act like they were your friend, but then stab you in the back? When we talk about people in relationships, there are a great deal of interesting patterns that come about. Stories about several heartbreaks that could have been prevented if people just communicated properly or let their intentions be known. This is not an all-male thing. Many females feel as though they get a bad rap. Many individuals are not having these developmental conversations. This issue is what leads to the next game, *Men Hear...Women Hear*. The purpose of this activity is to give individuals the opportunity to hear what each other has to say without being interrupted or being defensive. Essentially, I ask all the people who identify as a woman to stand in the front of the room. They are given about ten minutes to talk about men – they have the floor and can say whatever they want. Then I say to the men, who are sitting in the audience that their job is to sit there and listen. I wish you could see the looks on the people's faces in the room! Some faces light up and people are excited and some people moan and groan. It's fascinating to hear the different

112

concepts that women describe versus what men say. I want to give you a tidbit of what some of the women say during this activity.

I have the women go first, because like I said, I'm still a chivalrous man, but we'll talk about the real purpose a bit later. Typically, the men have sour faces, saying things like, "What do you mean we can't say anything?" I tell them to just hold up, they'll have their turn. The women then begin their part of the activity and the information begins to flow. They are saying that there is a double standard for men and women. If a woman goes out and sleeps with a bunch of people, she's a slut, but if a man goes and does it he's praised and high-fived. I even heard a quote about this, "A lock that's opened by many keys is a bad lock but a key that opens many locks is a great key." Women complained about men cheating, lying, and being dogs. The women often talk about men not listening, not knowing their needs, and being insensitive. They speak a lot about men blaming situations on woman's menstrual cycles. The women believe that it is because men are being insensitive and not really paying attention to women's emotions. The women talk about men having pride and not being able to see situations from women's point of view because they're too busy looking at it from their point of view. The women also talk about men just being too headstrong, never stopping to make plans, or being impulsive.

Then the conversation shifts almost right before the ten minutes are over. I assume that women have gotten everything out of their system that they needed to say. Usually one person says, "Well everybody, we all just need to hold up. It's not all men, it's some men." And then everybody chimes in with, "Yeah, it's only some men." Then the conversation shifts. Instead of talking about how bad men are, all the ladies in the room talk about how good men are. They share that their father is a good man or that their boyfriend's good to them – that not all men are bad. They say some men do listen, some men really do care, and some men really are considerate. Then, I promise you, almost like clockwork, the last minute or thirty seconds of this conversation, someone throws out, "But sometimes women…"

113

As if they didn't hear the original assignment, all the women completely change the conversation. Now they're not talking about men anymore, it's women talking about women and completely going off topic. But we will come back to that!

Now I allow the men to come up for their turn. Normally this happens one of two ways. Either the men are all fired up due to what the women said or the men just really don't have anything real to say. They'll just say women smell good, they look good, they're okay sometimes, and my mom's a woman and that's pretty much it. There are many different ways to combat this. It isn't normally until I pull both groups together that there are some real informative and intentional processing. What I mean by that is, when I bring both groups together I say, "What do you think about what each other said?" Many people say that they never really saw it from that perspective. We talked about perspective in a previous chapter – it's all in how you see things based upon your past experiences. All of those concepts are important. What we also learned from the two groups is that women sometimes attack other women or try and bring each other down. What we start to realize is that there are a lot of women that are also attacking women, sometimes worse than men do. There are certainly empowering women movements where women are encouraging and uplifting each other. You don't usually see a lot of men knocking other men down. So why does this happen with women?

A common theme consistently arises out of these conversations – individuals are hurt. They are hurting due to people or situations from their pasts. More commonly it is from past relationships. As we discussed in a previous chapter, pain is pain. It not only affects you emotionally, it can affect you physically and mentally. Unfortunately, to most people's detriment, it can change your entire outlook on life. What we start to notice is that hurt people, hurt people. Sometimes people can only meet you as far as they've already met themselves. People are still learning who they are. In this self-discovery phase, people they potentially care about can and will be hurt. This part of life is regrettable.

Imagine meeting people every single day who do not know who they are. They don't know what their self-worth is. There exist individuals who don't know what they want to do in life. They don't have any goals, ambitions, or values. They only learn what they're doing based upon their friends or what's happening on social media. You'd be surprised as to how many people out there fit this description. Are you one of them? This is not strictly reserved for those in adolescence; there are many adults that fall into this category. Imagine being 28-years old and not being mature or stable. You're not paying your own bills, you're not working towards a goal, just going wherever the wind takes you. Where do you find your grounding? Where do you find your purpose? When do you wake up and decide "I'm really going to get myself together?" Sometimes, it's all a matter of sitting down and really figuring out what I want to do with my life. Only you can bring yourself to this realization.

Sometimes this realization comes through a breakup or maybe through something like bankruptcy. Sometimes the reality comes through the loss of a loved one. As they say, the three greatest teachers in life are heartbreaks, empty pockets, and failures. These are the things that teach you the greatest and harshest lessons in life. These three teachers can be the hardest, but you can certainly pass the class. We notice that some people come into your life for a season and some come for a lifetime. You can't mix seasonal people with lifetime expectations. You also can't force people to stay in your life – staying is a choice. You've got to be thankful for the people who choose you for you! One day you'll look back and understand why it all happened. It takes a strong person to remain single in a world that's accustomed to settling for anything just to say they have something. Sometimes people won't even leave relationships because they feel it is their only option. I always speak up about relationships because I became stronger through the pain of a breakup. There were some days I had to get up and decide, "Today I'm going to make sure that I am happy and I'm doing it for me." I cognitively made a choice that I was going to exude positivity; not only in my life but also in the lives of others. I

115

always want to be a beacon of light or a servant to those who needed help; I want to have a servant leadership heart. I want to be able to have selfless care for other people, and of course self-care to keep myself whole. Everyone doesn't want that nor do they accept it. Not everyone is going to know how to handle you or receive your energy. That's not your problem. It's best for you to just make peace with that and move on because not everybody's going to appreciate who you are.

You've got to trust yourself. You've got to trust your heart. You've got to trust in your own abilities. Don't let mixed signals fool you. If people want to be with you they will, and if they don't, they won't. Indecision is a decision. You're only contained by the walls that you build yourself. Building a wall is a great thing; it keeps all of thenegative people out but it also keeps you trapped in. I remember when my wall was first broken; it was awkward for me to talk to people. I remember a woman came up to me and told me I was handsome. I had no idea what was going on and I responded with "Happy Birthday?!" Yes, that really happened. We've got to stop changing who we are for people who don't even know themselves. Ultimately the battle of the genders is a really interesting topic. It's one that students really love and we talk about the most often. Most importantly, we all realize that we have shortcomings, we're all works in progress, and none of us are perfect. We just continue to strive for what we think is best. We try to make sure that our basic needs are met and that we're all searching for this little sense of happiness.

Chapter 9
Well This is Just a Women's Issue

I had pretty prominent women in my life growing up – one of them being my mother. She's a very strong woman who didn't show you too many weaknesses. She wanted to not only be strong for her family but for herself. I have to give it up to the women, especially in this chapter. In case you couldn't tell, this chapter is all about women because women just go through a lot of unnecessary stuff in this world. Society makes it that women are second-class citizens. Depending on what type of woman you are, you could be lower than a second-class citizen. And I'm sorry, but I personally believe that America is more sexist than it is racist. Women have to go through hardships that men never will, yet men constantly and consistency comment on these issues.

Growing up as a man and seeing these hardships firsthand made me very sensitive to women's issues. I have two younger sisters. I was very close to my mom. I was very close to both of my grandmothers. I have aunts and cousins who are all women. They did not hide the fact that men need to be more sensitive and that men need to be quieter on issues that have nothing to do with them. That just because they're on their period, it is not a reason they respond so directly or are upset. Think about it, if you're a man reading this book, how many times do you hear any of the following on a daily basis: You're wearing that? You're overly sensitive. You'd be prettier if you wore makeup! Girls can't be on the team. Girls can't do that. It must be your time of the month. You just haven't found the right man. You're never going to get a man looking like that. You'd be so much prettier if you just smiled. What war on reproductive rights? She must have been asking for it. Calm down. Slut. Your clothing is distracting the boys. Your husband is totally whipped. Why are you getting so emotional? He picks on you because he likes you. You're too bossy. Stay at home parent...get a job! Working parent...why are you neglecting your kids? You're too

117

old to dress like that.

Come on now, men, when have you ever heard those things? You didn't and don't! Why? Because there's a double standard when it comes to women and men in America. If one man can destroy everything why can't one woman change that? Why can't one woman build everything? We have women in our own lives that had to protect their families by biting their tongues to preserve a man's ego. So, when we're talking about these issues, there are double standards in all things. There are double standards for women in the workplace. There are double standards for women in marriage. There are double standards for women in the type of careers that they choose. There are double standards for women in education. There are double standards for women when they're growing up in grade school. There are double standards for some women compared to other women. Sometimes it seems that women cannot succeed because something is always against them. And, if they can succeed, they have to work twice as hard to prove they deserved that success.

A big issue that is still facing women today, which people just don't want to talk about, is rape and sexual assault. As aneducator, I don't understand why we do not talk about sexual assault in grade school. It doesn't make any sense. We talk about sexual health education in K-12, but a lot of schools are trying to do away with that too. While the subject can be confusing to younger students, talking about sexual assault and rape to preteens and teenagers could create the changes we need. Of course it won't completely stop assaults from happening, but talking about consent could certainly reduce occurrences. Even the education is unfair for what we're teaching men and women. For example, we tell women: Don't go out dressed like that.Don't put your drink down. Make sure you go out with friends. Don't be flirty. Don't wear your hair a certain way. Don't seem like you're trying to turn him on. Don't, don't, don't, don't...DON'T! And what do we teach men? No means no. Boys will be boys. And then, we perpetuatethe misconception that sexual assault only happens to women when it happens to men as well. There isn't enough data to assess how much sexual assault is actually happening to men because most men are encouraged *not* to come forward or made to feel guilty about victimization. As a male, they don't want to become the butt of a joke so they don't come forward. Plus, there are so many people that question whether a man could be sexually assaulted. We have to remember that sexual assault is about power, not sex. Just because someone has a physical sexual response, it does not mean they consented. Underreporting prevents us from having accurate data. I mean, statistically speaking, we don't have 100% accurate data for sexual assault against women either. Many women don't come forward because they think that people will not believe them. They don't want to be retraumatized by telling the story or they don't want to be told it was their fault. That's terrible! What sort of society do we live in where women, who we claim we need and love, cannot come forward to say they have been assaulted, raped, or abused?

We need to teach our men that rape is rape; not boys will be boys. That there is no maybe when it comes to consent – the absence of a "no" is *not* a "yes." It doesn't mean try harder or buy her another drink. There was a rapist on a campus, who happened to be a talented swimmer that got three months in jail for assaulting an unconscious student. That is a major problem! We have judges saying more significant punishments would severely impact the rapist future. Well, what about that woman who was assaulted? What about her future – doesn't she deserve justice? It sets up a precedent for our young men and shows them that rape culture is acceptable. What if something like this happened to you, your best friend, or your sibling? Can we then all agree that it is not okay? But again, if it's not a personal issue, then it's not an issue at all.

I hear men talking about how women need to stay in their place that they need to do this or they shouldn't do that. How can you command this? Do you not have a woman in your life that you actually care about? Our current system and way of living cannot stay in place. Silencing of women is heartbreaking. I think that whenever women are speaking up about something, they're immediately silenced. If I'm in the workplace and I have

119

an innovative idea, people would say to me, "Wow, Justin is really going all out." or "Justin is really using his noggin' and really pushing us forward." If a woman speaks up to say something, then all of a sudden, it's "Well who is she trying to be?" or "That's ridiculous, where'd she even come up with that?" Suppose I come into work and I was dressed raggedy. People may say, "Justin must be tired from working so hard." If a woman came to work dressed raggedy, all of a sudden people would say, "Oh, she's not trying hard enough." These double standards have to cease to exist.

I think that behind every woman is a tribe of successful women who have her back. Real women are classy, strong, independent, loyal, and lovable. That's one thing about women that we have to recognize. We don't recognize their strength enough. When we talk about women, we always talk about meekness, weakness, or being submissive. No, no, no, no, women are strong, beautiful, fearless, and they are wise. We have to start changing the facet of how we view women. I am constantly reminded about how we just use women. We pimp them out every day by over sexualization. We can't even sell cheeseburgers without a woman being in tiny shorts or a bikini while holding a burger, worse yet, serving it to a man. When did you need someone in a thong to sell a cheeseburger? Even though Eleanor Roosevelt once said "No one can make you feel inferior without your consent." it still happens. You spend generations being told that you are less than and let me know if you feel inferior. Women have to put in extra effort to maintain their strength, dignity, and pride. It's terrible how we have to make women feel so incomplete just so as men can feel complete.

Even though people think about the feminist movement negatively, I don't believe all feminists are like that. People say, "They're too extreme, walking around burning their bras, saying that men are horrible." I think feminism is about the equality of everybody. If there weren't men in this world who were trying to downgrade women and make women feel less then, women wouldn't feel so incomplete. That's not to say that women need

120

men to feel complete, because they don't. There are a lot of strong, independent women that don't need men at all and just want to inspire people and aspire to be the best.

In this world, we have women living in constant fear. I remember when I told my friends that I went to another country by myself. My female friends said, "Man, that must be really nice to do that." I though to myself, "You have the money, and you have the time, why can't you go?" She said, "I'm a woman; I could never travel to another country by myself. It's not safe." I really didn't understand my privilege as a man until I understood that point. There are times that I recognize my privilege as a man. But then there are also times that I recognize I don't have privilege due to my Blackness. It's a shame that my friends can't do the same things that I do just because they're women. Then I think about my sisters, are there double standards that I have for them as women? Do I want them not to go to certain places or be with certain people? Yet, as a man, I could be with anybody I want wherever I want. No one questions me about the places that I go. No one questions when I go, who I go with, whether I leave my drink alone, or whether I'm going by myself. No one ever thinks about any of those things. Our women are queens and we have to treat them as such.

There are great deals of issues that women are dealing with on a daily basis. I reflect on the fact that women are always expected to compete with one another. We spoke about women versus women in a previous chapter. This is a reality for some women, especially in the workplace. Workplace discrimination happens, which in and of itself is terrible. But on top of that, women are forced to compete with each other for the little success and opportunities available for them. Women shouldn't be a default or an afterthought. They should be respected for what they can offer and treated fairly compared to their male counterparts. On top of that, why are we not consulting women in this country when we're making choices that directly affect them? Decisions are made on healthcare, health insurance, justice system, or even about the underrepresentation of women in politics. Women are mostly left out of these conversations.

We need to be going to the source. Women should be giving us insight in regards to the human trafficking epidemic, women in prison, health care, reproductive rights, and the wage gap. Why are we not inviting women to this table? How are men making *all* of these choices? Why do men get to make the laws about sick time, access to health care, or even maternity leave? We don't know what's going on with women who are sick, we don't know what's going on with a woman's body after they deliver a baby, or while they are pregnant. I think as a man, we need to understand that we cannot have life and life cannot be produced without women. Therefore, that alone just shows the power and significance that women have in this world. But again, their worth is not determined by reproduction.

Even with this, our issues are always the same: violence against women, rape, and sexual assault. Intimate partners sometimes cause these terrible scenarios; people that say that they love them but have the nerve to exploit them, abuse them, and treat them like objects. It's not even in the federal resources to convict the men who are doing this. Hundreds of men get away with it. When we look at the continuing gender wage gap, men are still making a good deal more money than women for the same exact job. I'm sorry, it's still a thing. I know anti-gender wage gap individuals will say, "Well no, it's because women are choosing jobs that are way below what men are paid." When I looked at the disaggregated information, I saw that most HR departments are made up of women. So you're saying that every single woman who's in HR have all conspired together to sit there and say, "Let's make sure that the women don't make as much money as men?" I don't think so. It doesn't happen that way.

When we think about the poverty, hunger, and homelessness, we only see men. They don't really show a lot of women who are homeless; it's just not a good look. But there are a lot of women who are, and this includes women with children. Usually, the caregivers, or people who give homeless people a place to live are women also.

I think about the treatment of women in prison and the

groping that occurs during the body search – that is sexual assault. Correctional officers are committing rape and it's not being taken seriously nor are they being held accountable. There are 75% more women who are taken into sex slavery and human trafficking than men. Why are we not speaking up for these issues? Is it because as men, it's not important to us since it's not happening to us? Is it because we devalue women? Is it because that as long as it's not happening to the women we love or care about, it's okay?

I think the biggest issue here lies with the underrepresentation of women in the political sector. Whenever you turn on the TV, you see cisgender men, most likely also heterosexual, white, and Christian. You don't see a lot of women in Congress. I think a shift is now starting to happen. We don't see a lot of women in politics, not because they don't want to be there, but because of barriers. We need women in there, representing and providing insight. We need them to be the ones making the laws. We need them to be the ones putting bills on the table because they're intelligent, strong, and fair. They should be the ones making laws about women's health and access to care. Men can't speak to this; men should remain silent on these issues.

There's even discrimination in academia in regards to how much female professors are making. Let's just look at the students – there are vastly more females in higher education. Yet, they still have to fight for equal rights access to resources. Look at the fields women are going into. People think that women are just going into nursing or education. There are plenty of women in math, sciences, and technology fields. It's really important that we highlight and show women that these areas exist for their future. It starts when they are born. There's a mold that is set up from birth. I said this before, when boys are born, they get the blue color and girls get the pink color. Those colors come with expectations. Women are supposed to be meek, kind, and nurturing. Women should smile, be hospitable, and act like a lady. I don't think that women should start acting like a lady until they're treated like a lady. Women are second-class citizens in America. The only time that I can recall in my history that being a woman was beneficial was when the Titanic was sinking and they let the women and children go first. That's pretty much it. And that was only the women and children that were in the upper class.

Women's interests are also devalued. Anytime a woman brings up something that's important to them, in society's eyes it's not important. We also criticize them for not being some ideal form of a woman that someone decided was true one day. They come in different shapes, skin tones, and sizes, with different hair textures, backgrounds, experiences, and sexual orientations. We can't expect all women to wear a size zero. A number doesn't determine your worth or beauty. All women are beautiful. Women don't need men to tell them that they're beautiful in order for them to feel that self-worth. That's why it's called self-worth. So women, if you're reading this text, I want you to know that your value is not based upon what society determines. Your value is not based on what others think, whether that is your crush, partner, parent, teacher, or whoever. Your value is based on you! We need women to start taking charge and start understanding their worth.

We can't expect some women to represent all women; it's not the same. Do I wish all women had the same attitude as a Beyoncé? Maybe? Because it seems like everyone always look at Beyoncé when it comes to the women empowerment movement. Look, this is not a shot at Beyoncé, and I know I'm going to get a lot of crap for this and I don't care; I'm going to call it like it is. I think Beyoncé is a great singer. I think she's a great performer. I think she's beautiful. I think she's definitely talented, and a great entertainer but that's what she is. She's an entertainer. I think that she truly does believe in the things she says and does but I don't think that she was really talking about any of these issues until she saw that she could profit from it. I think that when pop was popular, Beyoncé did pop. Then she saw the woman's movement was popular and moved to that arena. I don't think Beyoncé really started even talking about women issues or race until that became popular – then all of a

124

sudden she came out with *Lemonade*. Everybody started talking about how Beyoncé was so innovative. Ladies, was she innovative when she was talking about being "Bootylicious?" We've got to make sure that we're not relying on celebrities to speak for us because one set of women do not represent the rest. I'm not saying this as a shot to Beyoncé. No shade on the Beehive or Queen B!

There are a lot of different people that do this. They will jump on the bandwagon when something is important or popular. They will speak to the issues that you all think are important. Why are we waiting for people to speak for us? Why aren't we speaking out on issues that affect us on a daily basis? We need to all come together – not just celebrities, not just people that are empowered – it's about all of us.

The Women's March on Washington (and everywhere else that we marched) of 2017, had men and women show up. We had people who were transgender show up. We had people with disabilities show up. We had people from different sexual orientations, races, ethnicities, languages, and religions show up. All of those people are important. We, as the people, need to decide how this country is going to be. We, as the people, have the power. Yes, the government ultimately makes the rules and we in the end have to follow them, but it's up to us to choose who gets placed in those seats!

We went through the 2017 election talking about change, but did change really happen? Did people really come out? I think people fear change. I think change scares people. I think Hillary being in the White House and potentially being the first woman president scared many people. People fear the unknown. People fear what they don't understand. So they turned to a man they didn't fully understand. I don't have a problem with a woman being the Commander-in-Chief as long as she can do the job. The job of the President is to represent America, in the right way, not just their way. That's why I could never President because I would be too controversial. Why would you be controversial, Justin? I'm glad you asked! I would be controversial because I wouldn't make it about me. It's not about me. I think a lot of the times we ask these presidential candidates what their personal take is on issues. In my opinion, as the President you don't get the luxury to say what your personal opinion is; it's not about you, it's about the country. If it's not moving America forward, then it shouldn't be an issue. They're asked, "Well what do you think about this?" It doesn't matter what they think – what does America think? How is that pushing our country forward? We ask these presidential candidates all the time about their thoughts on marriage equality. Who cares about their opinion! They represent the opinions of the people, they don't get to just amplify their own beliefs. Are there LGBTQIA people in America? Yes! Do they deserve the benefits that they can only get from a spouse once they're married? Absolutely! Should they get the same benefits? Absolutely! Are they American? Yes! Do they deserve to have their union respected? Yes! Then, let us push it forward. What about these people who are illegal immigrants? Were they born here? Do they have families that want to come over here? Do we want to continue to make sure that America is the land of the free? Absolutely! Does that push America forward? Yes! Then let's do that. Moving forward has to be our main focus.

I know I'm making this issue short and sweet. I know there is a lot that goes into politics – the rules, the red tape, and of course lots of money. What I'm saying is, sometimes we just make things too difficult. We are so scared. It's not that deep. We do the same thing in student affairs. They say, "We've been doing it like this forever so we should just continue to do it like this." No people! We've got to change how we're doing things. It can't continue to stay the same way forever. If it stays like this, then, we get stuck. We wonder why the numbers of sexual assaults haven't gone down. We wonder why women don't feel that they're represented. We wonder why women don't feel like they're valued and why they don't think their worth is the same as a man.

We have to change our terminology. Our terminology is terrible. We chide men by telling them they throw like a girl, they're acting like a girl, and to stop whining like a girl. Those types of comments are insinuating that women are less than and that being compared to a woman is a negative thing. We can't teach our boys to talk like that. We can't teach our young men that this is okay. Again, let's go back to some of the other comments. Men, how many times are you told some of the things women hear daily? That your clothing or body is distracting your classmates or even your teacher? You're wearing too much makeup; you look like a clown. You men complain about anything. You're too skinny; eat a burger. You're too fat; eat a piece of broccoli. You'll want kids someday. Keep your legs together.

I get upset when I hear men say, "There are some issues that women go through that I am just glad I don't have to go through." That's not okay. I shouldn't be able to be on this sidelines of the issues and be okay with it. No, no, no, no! We need to be advocates for women. We need to be champions for women. We need to make sure that they are safe. We need to make sure that they are getting an equal say and equal pay. There needs to be equality all around the board. We, as men, cannot be the ones that say that. We, as men, need to shut up, take a seat and figure out what women need to rise up, then support it in any way we can. Keep in mind that they don't need us to succeed, but they need us to get of the way and give them a chance. People might be reading this thinking, "Justin is trippin'!" Sadly, I wish I were. When you've had someone special in your life that is female and they have been discriminated against due to their gender or have been passed up for opportunities because they're women, you need to say something. Or if you have woman in your life that hasbeen downgraded because they're a woman, or been assaulted because they're a woman, say something. It's no longer just a women's issue. It becomes an *everybody*issue. And, until it becomes an *everybody*issue, we won't be able to move forward.

I have done sexual assault awareness training at many universities. I think it's really important to talk about it. If you ever get an opportunity, you need to see the *Hunting Ground*, a documentary about rape on college campuses. It is going to

127

make you angry and sick to your stomach, at least that was my reaction – but you need to see it. It's about women who are trying to get an education and they've been sexually assaulted or raped. These institutions, that I am sure they are paying a lot of money to be at, didn't support them, and some didn't even believe them! I cannot imagine being assaulted, but then going to the people who are supposed to protect you, keep you safe, and fight for you, and they call you a liar. Even more disgusting and despicable, they try to cover it up to protect the institution's reputation. For that person to go through all of that pain of reliving the situation or becomingretraumatized just to be called a liar and not receive justice is heartbreaking. This is just abhorrent behavior by educational leaders. I think about some of these situations where the star quarterback raped a woman. They had entire stadiums boo her– all because she had hurt their precious quarterback's reputation. Look, I love football more than anybody. I'm a huge Philadelphia Eagles fan but if the they ever, *ever* allowed a sexual assault to be downgraded,erased, or be seen as acceptable, that would be the day that my jerseys went in the trash where they belong.

I took a gender studies course in undergrad. We talked about the women's suffrage movement, and I rememberthinking "Wow, that word sounds like women suffering." After that class, I learned that the suffrage movement was about women gaining the right to vote. As a society, if we don't know what's going on, we'll sign up for anything. We'll sign up for what we think is popular; we'll just jump on the bandwagon. One of my assignments for that class was to do a project on women's suffrage. I decided to walk around my campus with a petition to end women's suffrage; it was really fascinating assignment. I walked around with my clipboard and pen asking people if they supported ending women's suffrage. My position sounded good! Let me tell you, 151 people signed that petition to end women's suffrage. Just like Pokémon, got tocatch them all, all 151! Anyone will sign up for something that's good or at least what they think is good. All I did was go out and say, "Hey let's end women's suffrage; it's a terrible thing." And even though they had good intentions, ultimately, they supported the wrong thing.

I believe that's the same thing that happened in the 2017 election. I think that many people were scared and I think that many people were trying to do what was best for America, in their own way. Some people believe that if you voted for Donald Trump you are racist. I don't believe that. I think people made the best decisions based on their own knowledge. Come on, when you know better, you do better. Again, I don't think that people who voted for Donald Trump are racist. I just think that people who heard him speak so nastily and showed signs of misogyny, homophobia, Islamophobia, and all those other characteristics, just didn't find them to be deal breakers. Again, we have to ensure that people have the right knowledge and are knowledgeable before making these decisions. Regardless, women still have to persist even though they have all these odds stacked against them; they still have to move forward. They still have to continue to press on. They don't have the ability to say, "Well I'm just going to stop now."

If your dreams aren't big enough to scare you, then they're not big enough. Women are big dreamers and I love seeing women encourage, support, and empower other women. It needs to happen more. And now, we need to shift that. We need men to encourage, support, and empower women. Why, because we are all humans and we are all valuable – sex or gender shouldn't determine your worth in this society. Yes, we as men can help lift women up and encourage them, but women are strong enough to do that on their own. We just need to step aside and give them a fair chance. If we just keep making women fight to be heard or respected, we're wasting their valuable energy. Energy that they can be using to make a difference in this world instead of being wasted just trying to get a seat at the table. Just think, where would we be if women were at an equal playing field from the start? Would we already have a cure for cancer? Would there be an end to global warming? Would our people have access to resources they need to survive? Would the world be a better place? Limiting women's voices limits the possible outcomes too!

129

An empowered woman is an amazing being, beyond measure – strong, ambitious, and beautiful. As a man, I want to empower women. One day, if I have a son, I want him to empower women. I know, it's not men's responsibility to do this – women are powerful and self-sufficient. But I think it's important for men to be on their side, be their ally, and support them. We know women don't *need* a man; if anything men *need* women! I don't know if anyone else sees this the way I do because I know growing up as a Christian, we heard different. We were told "Well God made man first; he made a woman from a man." I just think it's so interesting how God made a woman. He didn't make women from a man's butt, so therefore we shouldn't just sit down and completely squat on all their issues. No, we need to treat them with the respect and dignity that they deserve. God didn't make women from feet, therefore we shouldn't be stomping on their ideas, dreams, and aspirations. God didn't make them from any other body part except for the ribs. The ribs are very important – the ribs are what protect all of the vital organs keeping you alive. This shows that we need women to keep us alive! We need women to continue to help the human race thrive. It's about time as a society that we really examine what it's like to be a woman. Sometimes as a man, it's hard to be comfortable in our own skin. We're taught our whole lives to be strong, don't show any tears, and be a man. Then, by the time we meet a woman (for those who are heterosexual), we hear women say "I wish I had a man who could show some emotion." By adulthood, we have already suppressed this in order to be masculine. It's the same thing for women.

We need to just be able to continue to provide solid and inclusive education. We need to be able to push women forward so that when a man tells a woman she can trust him, she can actually believe him and not be afraid. The fear that women have for men is disheartening. Men, don't you feel that? The fact that women are scared to walk at night because men are around, that doesn't bother you? It doesn't bother you that women have to walk down the street every day and get cat–called and treated as sexual object? Those things don't bother you? Well, if it doesn't, you're really enjoying the privilege of being a man. When you know yourself, when you'reempowered, and when you accept yourself, you become invincible; and there are a lot of invincible women out there! To the women that are out there doing the good work – standing up, speaking up, and supporting the movement – I salute you! It is not a job for the weary, weak, or faint of heart. I hope that you are encouraged and that you continue to do the great things you are already doing. We've got to do our part.

Chapter 10
Student Affairs Professionals –
Where Art Thou?

This chapter focuses on the direction in which student affairs is heading. I will be posing to the reader several questions that I often ask audiences when I am conducting training. Perhaps these questions will evoke some emotions about how you truly feel about your work within the student affairs field.

Like a lot of people in this field, when I was in college I had no idea I was going to enter student affairs. I started off as a Psychology major but ended up landing in Communications. As a Communications major, I learned a great deal about the business side of communications as well as marketing and especially public relations. This is what really interested me – the drive to get a message across and the ability to stand in front of people and publicly speak. It was exactly what I wanted. That major was made for me. Yet, I was still unsatisfied. Throughout my time as an undergrad, I had the opportunity to engage in numerous different student organizations. I worked with the Student Government Association and was a Resident Assistant for three years. I worked with student orientation and in the public relations office as a student leader. I was involved in a lot of student activities and probably every facet of the institution outside of my academic requirements. It came to my final semester of my senior year and it was time for me to figure out what I wanted to do for the rest of my life. Like a lot of students, I didn't know what I wanted to do. I had come to discover the harsh reality that I had gotten a degree in something I completely did not want to do. I couldn't see myself sitting behind a desk every day writing press releases. I didn't want to be on TV hosting shows. I didn't want to be a voice on radio. So, at this point, I had a worthless degree. Had I used my degree to my fullest potential, I could have gone out there and done anything I wanted, but instead I felt stuck.

Have you ever felt like that – putting all your hopes, dreams, passions, and ideas into something that didn't produce much fruit? I felt like a seedless tree. Like a tree that has grown to its fullest potential, but without seeds. If more seeds can't fall from the tree to the ground, then when that trees longevity is over, there is no new tree to blossom in its place. At this point in the game, I had no idea what I could do.

I was pretty close with the Director of Public Relations at Slippery Rock University and we had several talks; she was a great mentor of mine. I also had a great relationship with one of the Directors of Admissions. I remember them telling me that it was clear as day what I wanted to do for the rest of my life and that everybody could see it but me. I said, "Well what is it? What am I supposed to do?" I had no clue here. I had a full scholarship and I used it on a degree in something that I'm not sure I wanted to do long term. It was a great fall back but it wasn't something I was passionate about. It wasn't something that I could see myself really making a difference with and changing people's lives. They finally shared the secret that I was apparently missing. They said, "Justin, you've been involved in all of these different groups on campus. You definitely want to work with students for the rest of your life. You need to go into student affairs." I said, "Student affairs...what's that?" That is when I learned what this field was – supporting students, helping them through their journey, and encouraging the development outside of the classroom. I said, "Whatttt!?" It was like everything just clicked – the stars shone and my eyes lit up. I thought, all these things that I've been doing for my four years were not a waste. BINGO! That's exactly what I wanted to do. So that's how student affairs came about for me.

The door opened up for me to go to Indiana University of Pennsylvania – one of the top ten schools in the country for student affairs. Many of my professors had written the books that we were learning from. It was a high priority school that had a great reputation, a lot of networks, and really challenged their students. The program benefited me and pushed me to my peak academic potential. It was not an easy program at all – the

133

professors definitely did not accept subpar work. You had to really push yourself to your fullest potential. It wasn't one of those programs that you could sleep through. The program focused heavily on student affairs theory and practice, as well as outside of classroom internships and practicums. I was deeply immersed in the framework and the theories that back our practice.

After being in the field for a few years, I realized that 60% of my job hadnothing to do with theory or practice. But that more than half of the job, in the real world, was actually answering emails. How many of you feel like that? How many of you feel like the majority of your job is answering emails? Or going to committee meetings that could have been an email? When people ask what you do during the day, you say, "I answer emails." That's exactly how I felt. I started getting a different take as to what student affairs actually was. But really though, student affairs is important and necessary because these professionals are helping the students develop outside of the classroom. Academic affairs can only do that to an extent because they see students for 1-2 hours a day, if even that much. We see them for the rest of the time – in their social lives, when they're home, and when they are navigating the world. We're helping them with their development not only professionally but also personally. Overall, we're helping these students grow so that they can go out into the global society. Look at the type of students that we're getting. We have students that are told that they need to raise their hand before they go to the bathroom in K-12. Now we have them at college and we tell them, "Here you go, pick what you want to do for the rest of your life." Talk about mind-boggling! Is there anyone out there that is in the student affairs world that doesn't know what they want to do for the rest of their lives?I thought so!

We see where the students are developmentally when they arrive at college. So often I see students who are here because they are "supposed to be" or because their parents told them they had to go. They are here because it is just what you do after high school, after all, that's what all their siblings, cousins, neighbors, and so forth did. Many students don't even realize that you can find a lot of next steps without going to a four-year college, and that is perfectly fine. Students still even have false realities of college. Ridiculous things like, "If I get hit by a bus while I'm on campus, I'll get free tuition." or "If my roommate dies, I'll get a 4.0 that semester." Students, I'm afraid these concepts don't exist, they're urban legends. But, developmentally students need us and we need them. We have this crazy thing in student affairs called *in loco parentis*. Yes, we're in lieu of parents, but at the same time we are not these students' parents. Our job isn't to make choices for them but to help guide them so that they can make effective decisions for themselves. It's a difficult task in student affairsbecause you make strong, close bonds and relationships with students, but you need to let them figure some stuff out on their own.

Colleagues, think about this. If I asked you right now to pick your favorite student, what would you honestly tell them about the real world? If you could, would you shield them from it? It completely goes against our practice, but if you had the ability, would you exercise it? I know that we don't go out there searching for favorite students, but you know you've got them. You know, the ones that come in and make you feel like you're alive, like you are accomplishing your goals and making a difference. These are the students and the relationships that brought you into this field. If you came to this career to become a millionaire, you're definitely looking in the wrong place. No, we came into this because we care about the students. The students give us the drive and the passion to work the long hours and fight through the stress. We actually love our students and some of them we actually do refer to as our kids.

To me, student affairs has made big shift. The shift is that we used to be present to work with students – to help them learn and grow. Today, it seems like we're working *for* students not with them. What do you mean by that, Justin? Well, students paid their money and we're here to provide them services. We're no longer here to help them grow, develop, and become the individuals that are going to change tomorrow. No, they pay us

135

and were obligated to provide them with whatever they need. We are dealing with millennial students here – later millennials though, because I am also a millennial. These are the students that always had cellphones and didn't have to struggle through dial-up Internet. The majority of these students were born when iPads were already around, Wi-Fi is everywhere, and everything is available at the click of a button.

Most of these students feel very entitled – anything they ask for they should receive without hard work involved. This is the generation of participation trophies and you know what? We're also dealing with their helicopter parents who also think that we work for them as well because "they pay our salary." Funny, I've never seen a parent's name on my check, have you? Those sobering concepts can make any student affairs professional wonder why they got into the field in the first place. Many professionals unfortunately lose their passion because this new dynamic deters from our mission.

Let me ask you this: how many of you know someone in this field who doesn't belong here, or at least not anymore? I know that you all know somebody; that person who sits in that corner office and is supposed to contribute to student affairs initiatives but doesn't. There are people who have been riding the coattails of the institution, getting paychecks each week, but not providing anything new. This person is burned out. There are people who have been doing the same thing over and over again for the last twenty years. How dare you ask them to change anything! Yes, these people do exist. Those are the people that prevent us from having changes and innovations in our field. Oh God, not change at an institution...we've been doing it like this forever, we shouldn't change things. How many times have you heard, "I love your idea, I think what you said was very beneficial and I think it's something that we would love to incorporate. But, unfortunately, right now we do not have the budget for that." How many of you have heard "We've always done it this way, why would you want to change it? Why fix what isn't broken?" or"I know our student population is growing and the budget is decreasing, let's just stay the course."

Unfortunately, this is a sad but true reality for professionals in the field.

We sincerely need to look at this field from a new angle. We have higher student enrollment at most universities but fewer resources and smaller budgets to accommodate them. Quite frequently, institutions will call me to do professional development trainings. At one such institution, they were working with a model for the development and leadership of students that they've been using since 1994. Yet in 1994, this institution had 10,000 students but today it has grown to almost 25,000. If our students are changing and growing and the culture of our country is changing, shouldn't we be changing alongside them? Are we so hung up on institutional mission,goals, and outcomes that we can't see the need for change? The mission statements and the overall goals of our institutions should be progressing alongside the changes with our students, society, the job market, environment,and diversity in our country. The greatest resistance to change is fear. What if it doesn't work? Am I willing to take the blame for the initiative going south? My opinion is, if it doesn't work, you can always go back to the old model, but at least for now, try something new.

For those professionals in the field who are always complaining, have you made strides to change? If not, it's time you gave up your seat to those who really want to foster change in the institution. Again, what spaces are you making for change? If a student came to your office right now, would they feel that your office or your particular department welcomes diversity? Is it an inclusive environment? The value of any department is how it runs and operates with the students when the leader is not present. Without you at the helm, would your office fall apart? Again, I know we work at different types of institutions: private, public, religiously affiliated, large, small, and so on. Nonetheless, do your students carry the heart of your department and the mission of the institution? Or without you would your department even exist? Are you discouraged? If you answered yes to any of those questions, let me tell you, you're not alone with that feeling. If you're unsure why you got into the field in the first place, maybe it's time to reevaluate your purpose.

In the past ten years, I've traveled to almost 400 institutions and the complaints are still the same. I've even been to institutions that change their principals in order to increase enrollment. One institution I worked with was supposed to have 5,000 incoming freshmen, but by the spring they only had 2,800. So, they accepted anyone and everyone, just to meet the quota. The quality of their students dropped and, therefore, the institutional value and culture changed. The institution isn't even the same place because they lowered their admission standards.

You're saying that you're discouraged? Why? Is that because there's not enough money? There will never be enough money at any institution. In fact, right now, I'm sure somewhere at your institution they are finding a way to cut something. So, what are student affairs professionals, who are already not getting paid enough, supposed to do? And, now they're cutting your budget, which will require you to work more without extra pay. Many professionals feel as though they don't have support from their institution or even their department. To those reading who are managers or supervisors, do you really support the individuals who work under you or do they feel as if they are just another employee? Do you honestly know? Have you asked them?Can they come to you and tell you what's going on, not only professionally, but also personally? Or do the people who work for you, put on a mask and tap dance around in order to not ruffle feathers? Are you truly elevating the greatness of the people who work for you?

Student affairs professionals have greatness in them; they are multifaceted and talented. A lot of people who are in residence life also have an interest in multiculturalism. I know many individuals who work in career services but also own and operate their own companies. I know several professionals who work in student recreation, the student union, Greek life, admissions office, in the women's and gender equity, the LGBTQIA office, who all have outside interests. They all have additional roles with some aspect of higher education. Yet,

138

they're not allowed to do these jobs or talk about them at their own institutions. Why? You can't be a prophet in your own land. If we have in-house talent, why are we outsourcing presentations, workshops, and seminars that help encourage our students? The bottom line is: as student affairs professionals, we don't always support one another. One reason we don't support one another is due to over-the-top competition. Kirk Franklin, a popular gospel singer, posted on Instagram, "Humility is not born from insecurity but in the confidence of letting others go first because they can't take seats God didn't give!" All the time I hear: My proposal got accepted at this conference. I got this much professional development money. Look at all these side projects I'm doing. I'm on 12 committees. That's great! Congratulate them! Don't put others down. Our profession has one of the biggest water cooler gossip circles I've ever seen in my life. I've never seen so many people get talked about for doing great things. Student affairs isn't a competition. I know everybody's trying to reach the top. People focus too much on doing this or that so that they will be great. But, at the end of the day, are you making a change at your institution? Are you affecting students' lives? Those are the most important questions to ask yourself. Yes, we want to demonstrate that we are growing in our professional development in the hopes that one day, we can move up to assistant directors or directors. But that's not our main mission. That's not why we're here. We're here for the students. Have you lost sight?

We need supportive supervisors, but we also need to support one another! Most professionals I speak with tell me their successes are often looked down upon. I see a lot of people who get awards at conferences, are recognized regionally or nationally, and who are doing great work; yet their institution knows nothing about it. Why do they need to hold it close to their chests? Because to be great inside your job *and* outside your job means that people are going to despise you. They are going to be jealous of your success, after all, everything is a competition. Our students even notice this. Because of the relationship students have with professionals, they sometimes know more about your institutional culture than you do. They know exactly what's happening behind closed doors and it bleeds into our student body. We can't have that because our offices and our institutions are supposed to be safe havens for students.

For example, I remember having a conversation with a student from the LGBTQIA community who did not want to go home during spring break. The time came for us to close down the residence hall and the student said, "Justin, honestly, I'm not trying to be that person who gets fined, but do I really have to go home?" When I asked why this student didn't want to go home, they said, "I can't be myself when I'm at home. I'm gay. My parents don't accept it." I said, "Well home is home, right?" This is when I was still learning about some perspectives. The student said, "No, I don't consider my parent's house home. I consider this place my home." It was that day that I really understood that for some students, our institutions are more like "home" than their actual homes. For some students, we are their community. We are their backbone. We are their support system. Therefore, we need to keep institutional gossip to a minimum.

Some students don't have parental figures or adults to look up to, so we sometimes take on that role. I certainly understand *in loco parentis*, but the situation is what it is. We are dealing with complex students who have complex issues. But we can't lump them all together and treat them as though they all have the *same* issues. A lot of students have some really raw talent, but they need direction. As an example, I had a student on my floor that was causing trouble not only for himself, but alsofor every single person that lived there. Yet, he had a lot of raw talent. I finally sat down with him and asked him what he was involved with on campus. The student said, "I do absolutely nothing!" People, that's exactly why we are here!The student simply wasn't involved; he was floundering. I remember looking him right in their face and saying, "If you only used your powers for good, you would be an influential leader." This student went on to be the Student Government Association president and governed during his undergraduate career with pride, dignity, and excellence. How much are we intentionally guiding students

140

or are we simply issuing them citations over and over again without trying to get to the core of their behavior? Are we becoming so robotic that we know why students are coming into our office and we just give them what they want and push them out the door? How many students did you see today? Do you know their names? Do you know their backgrounds? Do you know where they're from? Do you know what their likes or their dislikes are? Or did you just give them an answer they could have easily found online on their own?

Some universities have eliminated student affairs departments from their institutions. The thinking goes along the line of we have websites and all these other resources. Do students really need us for their growth and development? Ask yourself that question because there's intention and intentionality. I told you before I am as a cisgender, heterosexual, Black male, and that means…I am like a unicorn in student affairs. Meaning, any time there's an issue with men they send them to me. Any time there's an issue with students of color they send them to me. Any time there's an issue with heterosexual students, they send them to me. Why? Is it because I can better relate to those students? In some situations, I do have a better understanding and dynamic with our students of color and sending them to me is a good idea. That's the ugly side of our field we don't like to talk about. Maybe sending that student of color to me was the best choice. However, it doesn't mean that my other colleagues are not as equipped to handle these situations. Can you imagine if every single time I had an issue with a student, I sent them to another office? There would be absolutely no way that people would be able to do their jobs. Just like there's no way I would be able to do my job. We have to go back to what's most important – student development.

We have to learn to not take ourselves so seriously. I remember very early on when I was a Resident Director, I really wanted students to listen to me. So, I tried scaring them; it didn't work. I tried giving incentives; it didn't work. I tried disciplining them; it didn't work. During my first year, students on the third floor of my building would trash it over and over again. No matter how much I whined, sent e-mails, had judicial conferences, met with students individually, caught them on camera, or gave them fines, the floor would still get trashed. I was the Director, I had all the power. They should listen to me, right? It wasn't until our custodial worker, Miss Sue, got involved that students actually listened. Why was that? As a Resident Director, I was perceived as the authority figure. However, Miss Sue paid attention to my students. She knew what rooms they lived in. She knew about theirclasses and their days. She asked how their families and pets were doing. The students saw how much work and effort Miss Sue put into keeping the floor clean that there was no way they would continue to trash that floor. Why? Because Miss Sue developed a relationship with them, they respected her and therefore, she had credibility. When she told them to not dirty up the floor and they didn't. It had nothing to do with power or authority. What does that show you? It conveys multiple things. It demonstrates that as student affairs professionals, sometimes we need to take a backseat and understand that as employees of the institution we work for, we *all* are responsible for students' growth and development. This is not just the responsibility of academic affairs or student affairs. Everyone, from the custodial worker all the way up to the president's office, have a responsibility to ensure these students are learning, growing, and developing. What else does it show you? It shows there are many people who are important at the institution that we overlook. When you see custodial workers at your institution, do you thank them? They work hard at their jobs every day, just like you! Maintenance workers, employees who provide the upkeep to the institution, same question, do you notice them? I know a lot of you probably complain about the IT services at your institution. Everyone probably thinks their institution's Wi-Fi is slow; it happens. Everyone thinks their dining hall food is tasteless; it happens. There are individuals who come in every single day, and they're not only serving the students, but they're also serving the employees. There's not one person who is more important than another. We are all in the business of supporting students.

142

As student affairs professionals, are we looking at our Black employees for knowledge and insight? I know sometimes my colleagues ask me questions as if I represent the entire Black community, as if I hold the answer to all of their questions. I hear, "Justin, I had a student who did this, what does this mean?" No, it doesn't work like that. Yes, there are times when Black colleagues and Black student affairs professionals have insights into the Black student population that our colleagues don't. Guess what? That's okay. Again, that's what we talk about, everybody being a part of the institution. At the same time, do not have your Black colleagues on speed dial just so you have a Black face or voice at your institution. I can't tell you how many times I've been put on a search committee so they can check the "diversity" requirement box. I've been on search committees that I wasn't even qualified for, but because I was Black, I met the quota.

This plight is something that most people of color experience not only inside their institution but outside of their institution as well. It's wrong that student affairs professionals, who have master's degrees and are supposed to be aware of their multicultural competence, come into the job and do the exact same thing that we're teaching our students not to do. When my white colleagues tell me, "Well you can't feel like that because it didn't happen like that." Essentially, what they just told me is everything I just said is wrong, so shut up. Student affairs professionals, listen to me. It's very important that when your colleagues of color are speaking, you try very hard not to invalidate their experience. Just because you didn't go through it, you didn't hear it, and you didn't experience it, doesn't mean it's not true. We need you to be able to support everyone at our jobs. If I perceive it, then it's my reality. Please don't invalidate the experiences of your colleagues of color, those with different sexual orientations, religions, and so on. When you argue that it happened like *this*, not like *that*, you are just expressing how *you* experienced the situation. In that process, you are overriding the experience of someone else and canceling out their feelings. Everybody experiences things differently and everybody has to

143

know their role and power. Do you know how many times I've talked to students at the end of the semester and they told me they are transferring? When I ask them why, they say, "Well director such and such said this to me, and I can't stand this institution." Do we truly recognize how important our words are when we speak to students? We're planting seeds that can grow for the rest of their lives.

In chapter 1, you read how my high school counselor planted a very negative seed, but out of that negative seed, I was able to blossominto a tree of success. Many people unfortunately carry these negative seeds for a lifetime because they don't have the resources or support to turn the negative into something positive. I've had many situations where I just acknowledged students and said hello to them, very much like most of you do. Then later on, that student comes back to me and says, "Thanks, you made my day when you spoke to me." There was a student I had once who had cerebral palsy, and I'll be honest, I had a very hard time understanding the student verbally because the palsy had affected her speech. What would normally be a three-minute conversation was now a 25-minute conversation because it took that long for her to convey what she needed to say and for me to properly understand her. But, I intentionally took the time with that student and it made all the difference. She later came back with a letter that she wrote to me describing how important she felt at that moment and that at no other time at the institution, did she feel as if anybody took her seriously. She felt most people just patronized her by nodding their head at her and smiling. Take the intentional time. It works wonders.

Students don't need us to always tell them what to do. We're here to advise students, to point them in the right direction, and to give them a gentle push toward their destiny. We have to pay attention to our student's needs and wants first, but they are not our pet projects. Some of our students are actually spoiled and it would be helpful if we allowed them to figure out problems on their own, instead of handholding.

Some of our Black students feel as though white professionals don't care about them. Do they feel that way because it's true? Absolutely not! Well, if that's not true, why do students feel that way? The majority of the people in our profession care the same way about all of their students. As student affairs professionals, you have to stop owning things that have nothing to do with you personally. I hear, "Well that student doesn't like me." It's not about you – it's about the culture your office is cultivating and portraying. And if the problem lies in the culture of your office, you have the power to change that!

For example, I remember speaking with the Director of Residence Life at a particular institution who was frustrated that he could not recruit students of color. He said, "I don't understand it, Justin. We go to their offices of Multicultural Affairs, and we tell them about this great job. I take time out of my own schedule to go down there; yet, nobody ever wants to be a part of our department even though they get free room and board! I don't understand why we can't recruit students of color!" So I asked him, "How many students of color do you have on payroll right now?" He said, "Well, in our department, out of 121 students, we have five students of color." I said, "Oh, that's interesting. Have you ever talked to those five students of color about their experience in your department?" He immediately replied "No." I said, "So you don't know what their experience is like?" He said, "No." again. I then asked, "What you're offering is a great opportunity and very generous at that! And so they should be so lucky to have it, right?" He paused and said, "Well, I didn't mean it like that." We then talked about the difference between intent and intentionality. I assured him "I know you didn't mean it like that. I know that's not where your heart is. But, look at what students are seeing:"'Hello everyone, I'm part of Residence Life and you should be a part of it because you're Black.' That's not what you said, but that's what they heard."

In addition to the harmful messageswhich sometimes emanate from our offices, even messages that are meant to be positive but are perceived negatively, sometimes past experiences students of color have had are transferred to us. It's

145

not about you personally. Many students of color are coming from areas where they experience racism, prejudice, and discrimination on a daily basis. It's only natural these students would bring those experiences with them to the institution. If students can't trust authority in places they call home, what makes you think they can trust authority on our campuses? It has nothing to do with you. It has to do with the experiences they already had. If you want to do something about it, change their perception, go the extra mile to impact a student's life. Take the initiative! Don't expect the students, who have less power than you, to make the first move. Most professionals don't take the initiative. They say, "I feel uncomfortable." or "I don't know how to relate to those students. Those students don't come and talk to me." If those students don't come and talk to you, go talk to them! At your institution, where are all the students of color hanging out? How often are you there? Are you present or even remotely visible? Do they know who you are? Do they know what you're about? If they don't, you don't have any reason to complain *and* you're part of the problem. I think it's so funny when I see staff members with diversity stickers on their door claiming their offices are safe spaces; yet, no diverse students are ever there. We need to evaluate what those stickers are actually supposed to symbolize. It is not so much what our colleagues are doing, but more so, the attitude in how they are doing it. Attitude is everything.

In order to be involved in students' lives, we also need to recognize new trends that students are participating in, especially new technology trends. Our students are constantly interacting with new technology and gadgets. As I am sitting here writing, I am also playing with a fidget spinner, the latest toy craze. There's a new fad, app, dance move, clothing style, food, and Netflix show almost every day. It is a good idea to follow these new trends; it might make you more relatable. It's not a "young people's thing." Take an interest in what our students are engaged in, even if you yourself could care less.

Being relatable creates a relationship with students and through that relationship, growth and development occurs. This growth and development occurs for us too because through our experiences with students we become better professionals. It's a very simple equation. If you can meet students where they are, they can grow, develop, and mature into the citizens the world needs. We have to get out of this mentality that I can come to work from 9:00-5:00pm and then live my own life. Yes, we have to have balance between work and home; yet, you can't pretend those students don't exist when you go home. I know student affairs professionals who work at predominantly Black institutions that come from the suburbs, do their teaching, do their training, and then go home. They make no impact on their students. They're just there to give them the required material, and that's it. I also know people who are supposed to work 40 hours each week, but they're working 60 or more hours. Why? It is because they care?How many of you know, and it may be you, professionals who are working far more hours than they are putting down on their timesheet? You are putting far more time into the students than you are ever going to get paid for. While that is noble, it is also a problem. It is on us to maintain work life balance so that we don't burn out. The best type of relationships I have with students is when I am authentic and real. When I was sad, I was sad. When I was mad, I was mad. When I was happy, I was happy. Yes, I remained professional, but I also showed students that I was someone they could relate to. I wasn't a fake. They respected that and they grew from that.

Unfortunately, a lot of individuals do not have sufficient multicultural competency. I talk to a lot of professionals who say they never had to take a diversity class while in their student affairs or higher education program. They never had to discuss issues of multiculturalism, cultural awareness, or diversity. How are our institutions allowing student affairs professionals to earn degrees without talking about low-income or first generation college students? What about our international students, students of color, and those with language barriers. Most people tell me they talked about students with different sexual orientations but never talked about the high sexual assault rate that some of these students may experience. Their understanding is so basic, it's

147

frightening. The only time they discussed students with disabilities is when referencing physical limitations, not mental illness nor learning disabilities.

Multicultural offices should not be the only offices on campus that work with diverse students. They are too numerous to be addressed by one office. And there's a danger in only having one source of information. When students only get one perspective and it creates a reason for certain students to only trust the opinion of that office. In truth multicultural issues are multidimensional and need to be addressed from various angles and different perspectives. Everybody should be working on diversity; however, this work is not easy, and it is usually only accomplished by a few. For those in the struggle, I understand. It's emotionally draining to be expected to not only fix every race-related incident on campus but to also educate the unenlightened. For example, most multicultural offices say they can't get white students into their offices. What kind of story is your office telling versus what kind of story is the white student actually hearing? Is your space free and open for everybody? Everyone says that it is, but is it truly for *everyone*? Is it a welcoming and inclusive area? I understand that sometimes it can't be. Our students of color do need a space where they can find strength, counsel, and family. However, we can't be the first ones pointing the finger when white students don't show up.

We need to give students multiple perspectives. We need to ensure that we are staffed with diverse professionals. I often think about how many teachers of color I've had in higher education. Let me tell you, I can count that number on one hand. Out of the approximately 100 classes I took during my undergraduate and graduate education, I probably had two professors of color. You think the students don't see this as well? Whenever I do see someone who looks like me at work, I have a Celie and Nettie patty cake moment from *The Color Purple*. Please look this up if you don't know what I mean. When Black professionals work in an institution, we're Black professionals. We have knowledge, and students respect us. When we go out into the real world, we're just Black. People don't look at us and say, "Oh that person's educated." In fact, more times than not, when I tell people I have a master's degree, it's almost as if they want me to prove it. Or, they're just stunned and say, "Oh wow! You're very educated. I didn't know that!" As if my skin color determines my educational level.

Do your students see you in the community? Does the community embrace you? A lot of our students of color belong to many different student groups: Latinx organizations, the Black Student Union, LGBTQIA student service centers, and everything else. Do they see you come to their programs? Do you go to their late night programming? Are you an ally? And before you answer, remember, being an ally isn't just having that little sticker on your door that says "I'm for LGBTQIA rights." or "This is a safe space." Being an ally means you have a call to action to do something. Saying you're an ally means nothing; you have to *be* an ally! BE PRESENT! Think about it. I could tell you I'm a dingo or a walrus; does that mean that I am a dingo or a walrus? No, because nothing has changed about me. Change needs to happen on the inside before it can be reflected outwardly.

We have to handle our defensiveness. Do you know how many times I try to talk to people about their understanding of diversity or their multicultural competence? They're always quick to say, "Well, I understand this because I went to a diversity training...once." or "But I have a Black friend!" We need to process constructive feedback and not become defensive. As a diversity trainer, do you think I say and do everything right? I am constantly checked and corrected, but it's alright, people are making me better. Iron sharpens iron. On the other hand, I had a colleague once who used to say, "You got to eat the meat and spit out the bones!" In other words, if it doesn't apply to you, don't worry about it.

If you realize you need to up your multicultural competence IQ, are you participating in webinars to help you do this? Are you looking at case studies so you can help mold your institution? It's all about sharpening your multicultural skills. I understand there aren't too many theories dealing with

149

multiculturalism in our field. I also understand that most of our theories are gathered from different fields of study. None of that matters! We have to use the theories that we know and incorporate them into why we do what we do. Theory into practice people! Besides basing our practices on theory, we need to also rely on the experience and knowledge of others. If I don't know something, I'm going to ask a professional who is competent in that area. For example, I may have a student who comes to me who was sexually assaulted. I have never experienced this, so I should talk to one of my colleagues in gender equity or the women's center. This will allow me to gain better insight and understanding so I can assist my student beyond referring them to resources. Be friendly with other departments and offices. You need them and they need you!

Many schools have asked me to do "diversity audits" or "campus climate surveys." I'll travel to an institution and talk to the president, the president's board, and to the president's cabinet. Then I'll go and talk to all the student affairs offices; that's where I learn about all the dirt that happens at the institution. Keep in mind, the issues I've been discussing are ubiquitous across campuses all over the country; they aren't confined to one institution. The majority of these issues come up at most institutions. After I talk to everyone, I devise suggestions and an improvement plan for the institution to create a more accepting campus climate. Some institutions implement these suggestions to create a more inclusive environment. Some of them don't follow through.

Our research and assessments show that students want to feel as if they belong at an institution. They want to know they are more than just a number. They want to feel as if they're at homeand that they're accepted. They don't want to go somewhere where they're just spending their money. At the same time, we don't want to give them participation trophies they don't earn. We have to give the students what they paid for and what they paid for was to grow and develop.

We've got to stop looking at the numbers. We've got to stop saying, "Well if I offend a student, they'll leave and if they

150

leave, our institution won't have any money." I get it, there is pressure coming from above. In order to keep the institution's doors open, you have to keep the students enrolled. I've seen shifts in student affairs where students are now getting three, four, five or even ten alcohol violations, yet the students are still enrolled. Are we teaching our students that if you break the law, you're going to get ten chances? Are we teaching our students that they can do whatever they want and that there are no consequences? That's a dangerous lesson, and we're the ones teaching it.

We often talk about our students of color transferring. Why? Our students of color are transferring because some feel our schools don't support their culture or that they aren't accepted. Now *that* is an issue! Can you comprehend a student thinking they need to transfer because a school doesn't represent or support their background? What does that mean? It means that we might need to start going to different areas to recruit students. Students need to see other people that look like them on college campuses. This is not solely for students, but professionals as well. We might need to change how HR recruits professionals of color. Sometimes, it's hard to find footing at an institution when the surrounding areas are devoid of diversity.

For example, as a Black male attending, Slippery Rock University, there were no places where a brotha could get a haircut. I had to rely on other Black students to cut my hair, or drive an hour to the nearest city. Often times, I had to contemplate and map out how long I could go without a haircut. In western Pennsylvania, stores label hair care products for Black people as the "Ethnic Hair Care Section." In the Philadelphia area, all haircare products are stocked together, minus the categorization. So not only do students of color sometimes feel as if no one on campus understands them, this feeling is compounded by the lack of diversity in the larger community. Can you get a better understanding as to why some students don't feel at *home*?

How can we help them feel at home? Well, we have to provide an environment where people love and care about them.

151

We have to provide an atmosphere that makes them feel comfortable and at home. And, we have to provide them with the tools and resources that students can use and in turn, learn from. Are we too sensitive? Are we not sensitive enough? How many of your colleagues actually call you out when you say things that are inappropriate? I hear male colleagues saying very inappropriate things to our female colleagues. Yet, nobody calls them out. Why? Are we afraid of workplace retaliation? Are you afraid to go to HR? God forbid we have to go through sexual harassment training. We talk about how our guiding principles are the foundation upon which student affairs was created and how they are the groundwork for what we do. Maybe we are blindly following them without looking at what's really going on in front of us? How are you transferring your theory to practice if we're unaware of what's presently going on and pertinent to our students.

Every institution has a different makeup and personality. I know not everything in this book will apply to everyone reading it. I also know that a lot of you are reading this and are saying, "Wow! He's hitting it right on the head!" Maybe you're saying, "Man, Justin's really going hard on white people, didn't he already have a chapter on white privilege, geez!" Regardless, if the shoe fits, wear it. This chapter is about self-examination. This goes for everyone. These are examples of crucial issues we need to talk about in student affairs, yet, no one is talking about them. When you're in your divisional meetings, are these questions and issues in the forefront of the conversation? Is this what we're assessing? Is the data that we're gathering from our students truly accurate? Am I even growing in my job or is my desk just collecting dust? Supervisors and managers should be consistently challenging, evolving, and growing professionals. I know this to be true because I have a supervisor who does this for me. I am constantly amazed by her ability to pull out the best in others and me in the field. If this isn't happening for you, something needs to change.

All that being said, there are some common questions that student affairs professionals ask me and I would like to talk about them. One question that I get often is, how should student affairs professionals challenge racism and discrimination? The first thing you need to do is actually become aware that racism and discrimination exists. Are you aware of the discrimination that happens on your campus? Or are you not aware of it because it doesn't happen to you?Institutionalized racism is a thing. Student affairs professionals need to take a step back and get a clear view of the experiences of *all* of our students. I've done trainings at schools where the student conduct department is being sued by students of color because they feel they are receiving unfair treatment; that the charges against them are harsher compared to white students who are engaging in the same behavior. Is this happening at your institution? Do they even know who to go to in order to report injustices? Just as there is a large gap between actual incidents of sexual assault and reported incidents, there are far more incidents of racism and discrimination on our campuses than we'll ever know. One reason incidents of racism are underreported is because students don't know who to talk to about it. Another reason is they feel as though nothing will be done about it even if they do report it. Probably the best solution is to invest in bystander intervention training. We're all bystanders. We're all responsible for our fellow human, and we're all responsible for the climate on our campuses. If you hear someone using language that isn't inclusive or telling a racist or sexist joke, call them out on it. We have to challenge people. We have to be willing to help people grow. As a bystander, as a witness, we are responsible for incidents that are happening on campuses, without necessarily being the person who is causing it. We all have to intervene. If someone says an inappropriate word, we have to challenge it. If someone is engaging in inappropriate actions, we need to talk to them about it. If somebody is creating a culture at the campusthat is not reflective of our mission, goals, and values, we have to change it!

Student affairs professionals ask me how do I create inclusive environments? My response is: are you really listening to what students are saying? You might send out a survey and

153

get a few respondents, but are you actually incorporating their suggestions? Furthermore, students don't care about emails. If your main means of advertising are posters and e-mails, you're failing! Students get so inundated with emails and ads, they have become obsolete. Think about your common bulletin board. It looks like a Staples store threw up on it! Students are not reading those ads! And, guess what? Neither are you. We're spending a lot of money and killing a lot of trees for nothing; talk about zero sustainability. The average student is getting about 60 emails a day. They're not reading your e-mail about your program that's happening two weeks from now. If it's happening two weeks from now, students don't care until about three hours prior to it starting. For the most part, our students are only attending programs if we're giving out condoms and pizza anyway. We need to change how we're going about marketing our programming efforts.

When you're talking about inclusive environments, do your students feel as if they're part of the community? Is there someone they know they could go to if they have a problem, a professional? Right now, I'm sure you can probably think of five students you know by name, but you might not know about their family or their hobbies. You might not know the things they're struggling with or what kind of week they've just had. Those are the things that students want to share in an inclusive community. Yes, sometimes it's awkward. Sometimes our students don't understand why we're talking with them. They might think it's a little weird, especially if you've never really had a conversation with them before. If, however, you make those efforts from the beginning,initiating a conversation with them later will seem more authentic. You could approach a student and say, "Hey, I noticed you come by my office a lot, but I never got your name." When they reply with their name, that's the start of a personal dialogue. Invite them back with a, "Next time you stop by the office, I would love to chat." This action plants a seed. We talked about what happens with seeds of negativity and seeds of positivity. Those seeds of positivity are the reminders that someone really wants to talk to them. You would be very surprised at the number of students who would take you up on your offer. Do you go to lunch with students? Do you show up at students' programs and not just sit in the back? If you're not there to interact and be a part of the program, don't go! You're sending more of a negative message by doing nothing than not going at all. You have to be integrated into their lives; you have to be active; you have to be there! That's how you create inclusive communities.

As a diversity trainer, it's interesting to go through diversity training with some of my colleagues. I've had colleagues say to me during training, "Justin, I'm just so sorry for my whiteness." As if I can be responsible for that! They say, "I don't see you as a color Justin, I just see you as you." Like I woke up this morning and figured out for the first time that I was Black. I have a lot of white colleagues who ask me, "As a white student affairs professional, what can I do to support my Black colleagues or students?" It's called just that; support. You might not understand it, but just try to be empathetic and listen. You might not have ever gone through whatever it is they have, but be empathetic. If there is a racially charged issue in society and it is bleeding into your campus, think about what you say before you say it. Take a step back and think about someone other than yourself. That requires you to not be selfish. Again, support means much more than putting a sign on your door with a slogan. It may mean going to a student affairs colleague and saying, "You know, I can't comprehend what you and the community were feeling when Trayvon Martin was shot and killed. I don't understand it, but if you feel comfortable and wanted to talk about it, I'm here to support you. I'm here to listen; I'm not here to tell you what you should feel. I'm not here to tell you what you should do. I just want you to know if you ever want to take time to help me understand, I would be open to that."

Student affairs professionals, know that it is not your Black colleague's job to come in and educate you. It's not our job to inform you about all things "Black." It's not our job to consistently give you professional development every single time something happens. Black professionals are T-I-R-E-D; we are exhausted! We can't be responsible for our own growth and development and your growth and development too. It's going to take some effort on your part. As student affairs professionals, if you mess up, own it; don't make excuses for why you said something or did something. Sometimes professionals do things that are offensive. Guess what? It happens! As Black student affairs professionals, we sometimes do things that are offensive as well. Black professionals have to own up to it too! When you make a mistake, own up to it! Say, "You know what, I'm sorry. I stink right now and I'm going to try to do better in the future." Own it! Make amends! Move forward! Grow from the experience! If you're not growing as a student affairs professional, you are wasting your time.

People ask me all the time, what do I feel is the biggest problem in student affairs? That's a very loaded question. I think there are a lot of issues in student affairs just like in any other field. I do believe, however, that one of the biggest issues is many of our offices are siloed. Some institutions have multiple departments such as the women's center, multicultural office, LGBTQIA, and so on but only collaborate on one program once a semester. We have to stop this! For example, if there's an issue in regards to female students, don't just immediately send them to the women's center. No! It's everybody's responsibility to make sure we are educated about issues that affect our female students. Too often we refer students and bounce them around from office to office. Yes, some issues need to be dealt with by specifically trained professionals, but handle what you can. Just don't push students out of your office because you don't want to deal with the issue.

Another common thing is if there's an issue relating to our students of color, they are just sent to the multicultural office. No! You should be equipped and skilled enough to handle a student issue regardless of race, gender, background, sexual orientation, religion, culture, or ethnicity. We are too quick to transfer students to another person when an issue comes up that we are uncomfortable with. Students don't like that and neither

156

do parents. I know of an institution that doesn't allow you to transfer calls; you're just not allowed to do it. When a parent or student calls, you have to ask them to hold on while you get the answer for them, instead of transferring the call. Nobody likes to be transferred! You want the answer from the person who picked up the phone. Are we doing that? Are we taking the time to really get to know what other offices are doing? Or, do we only know what the other offices are doing when we get a newsletter or mass email listing all their projects and programs. Not that it matters since most of us are deleting those emails without even reading them! We don't even support other offices' initiatives. We only show up to their programs when there's food. Or, we only show up to their programs when someone comes to our office and gives us a personalized invitation; as if we're so high and mighty in our department that we require a personal invitation or we won't go! We can't have ironclad boundaries that prevent us from collaborating with one another. We need to have permeable boundaries that allow us to be involved with other departments on campus to work together for the good of the students.

We can't assume professionals from other offices only have one skillset in their tool bag. Just because they work in residence life, doesn't mean they only have knowledge and skills related to housing. Just because they work in student activities, doesn't mean they only know how to put on programs. Just because they're in student recreation, doesn't mean they only know about staying active. Many of our colleagues are talented and skilled in many different facets of student affairs. We need to remove the stereotype that people only know one thing and that they're only well-versed in one area of expertise.

I would say another big issue in student affairs is that both academic affairs and student affairs do not work with each other. We must efficiently work together in order for institutions to be successful. Individuals in student affairs have a negative attitude about academic affairs. They think academic affairs personnel are a little stuck up and that they don't want to work with us either. I get it! Somebody has got to lay down the weapons and say, "Look, in order for our institution to work to its fullest capacity, we need to work collaboratively." In fact, models show that academic affairs and student affairs divisions that work well together increase enrollment, retention, and graduation rates. Isn't that our goal as an institution? However, this requires both offices to meet in the middle. Academic affairs professionals have their stereotypes about us as well. Some of them believe student affairs professionals are glorified babysitters. Some believe that we only play games with the students or should not be taken seriously because we are not part of the academy. I've even been told that people in the academy don't recognize our field because they believe we hijacked our theories. They say we take theories from other fields and apply them as our own.

We have to make the effort to bridge the gap. Right now, you're probably thinking, "I've made an effort. I've tried to get them to collaborate together." TRY AGAIN! If you work in academic affairs and you're reading this, you have to work together with student affairs. We are not professional babysitters! We are not carnival workers! We're not just creating flashy programs so that our students are happy! Sure we do that, it's part of providing an engaging and fun experience for our students, but that is a small portion of our job. We need to change how we perceive our student affairs professionals. What do you think student affairs professionals are doing? When you ask people about their profession, they tell you what they do. For example, if you asked a baker what they do, they would say, "I bake; I'm a baker." When you ask someone in academic affairs what they do, they say, "I teach; I'm a teacher." What do you think student affairs people say? Well, we say, "We teach as well." We may not be teaching a standardized curriculum with a syllabus, but we're certainly educating our students. Our teaching comes from programming models. Our teaching has learning outcomes, and our teaching is designed toeffectively assist student's growth and development as active members of society.

The last question I get asked in student affairs is, "How do you bring your students together? We see you traveling, we see you've developed these programs, how do you do it? We don't have that same community here at our institution. It's really difficult for us to bring our students together, what can we do?" My answer to that question is, what sort of space do you have to allow students to come together? Student unions don't cut it. Are there spaces where you see diverse students hanging out? No, there probably isn't. When I conduct the Diversity Awareness Program, my job is to create a space and I only get a two-hour window to do so. I can't have individuals engage in the program without making a safe space where everyone feels as though they can contribute and not feel judged. Creating an inclusive environment does not take much time and effort. It takes people who are passionate about it and who have the right attitude. It takes effort to make sure students are having fun, that their voices count and that the environment is free of shame and judgment. Are they in an environment where they can say whatever they want, but they must say it respectfully? Everybody wants to have fun! We can mix our learning outcomes, values, and institutional mission and have fun doing it.

Students love interactive programs. Students like to be part of something bigger than themselves. I've done this for ten years, and it can be done. Students don't want to sit down and be lectured; they get enough of that in their classes. They want to be able to use what they've learned, their experiences, and the things they know and be able to tell people, "Hey, I know a little bit about this or hear me out." and "Hey, I went through this as a child." They want to share what their parents and their religious organization taught them. Having everyone bring their knowledge and expertise to the table is much more effective than lecturing about this or that from a PowerPoint presentation. That model of teaching has to go. Why? Our students don't learn that way anymore. Secondly, many students have different learning styles. So, if we're only using PowerPoint as a way of learning, you're forgetting those students who need action to learn, students who need to learn audibly, or students who have learning disabilities. Different learning styles should be taken into account so our students can learn and retain the information. Where are your strengths? Are you using your strengths and skills to the fullest capacity? Does your institution even allow you to do that? If your skills are weak, what actionable steps are you taking to improve them? All of these things take place when you are trying to bring students together. They see it people! And, they're relying on us to do better.

Now that you've read this chapter, how have you been challenged? Now that you have finished reading about this topic, what can I do to improve? You can either continue to live the life that you're living, or you can make a change at your institution. It's on you. I hope I challenged or inspired you, even just a little bit. What I do know is this – above all else, our ultimate goal must be to develop and grow students, together. Go out and have some conversations with colleagues you do not know that well. You will be pleasantly surprised by what you hear.

Chapter 11
My Final Thoughts

HOORAY! You are the real MVP, you made it until the last chapter, nice job! I know that some of you probably jumped right to this chapter because you heard me say, "If you're looking for encouragement during your day, run to this chapter." I am literally putting my heart on the page here people.

For those who are looking for a summary of the book in this final chapter, I'm sorry, but you will not find it here. To conclude this conversation about diversity, it would imply that diversity could be concluded or have a finale. This simply isn't the case. Diversity is fluid – it is constantly changing and evolving. We as individuals need to be able to fully adapt and change with it. Instead, I chose to use this final chapter to incorporate life lessons.

Life lessons are essential, and trust me, I have a lot of them. Many of you will read this book through a very critical eye. Several of you, who have much higher degrees than I have, at the moment at least, may be asking, "Where is the theory, where is the research, where is the data that supports all these things that Justin said throughout the book?" This book wasn't about that. This book is about all of my experiences, my thoughts, and my heart. It is about the conversations that I have had with students, faculty, and staff, as well as the things that I've seen. This book is about putting all that on paper to share with you. People have encouraged me to go out and speak, to go out and write, and to push my message through other means. That's what this book is – a culmination of those delivery channels, all rolled into text.

This book wasn't written to shape the very foundation of student affairs. It isn't to tell you about some groundbreaking new theory or some new assessment tool that was going to change the whole facet of our field. This book is for everyone – student affairs professionals, educators, students, that person who heard about my experiences, and anyone who wanted to learn something new. I want you to be encouraged. I want you to know that there is someone else out there that understands you and values your feelings and ideas. That's where this book came from. This last chapter is just really going to be spoken from my heart. As I'm writing this, I'm thinking about the encouraging words that were given to me and those that I have given to others. Honestly, this last chapter is almost like a sendoff. If you made it this far in the book, great! If you just picked up the book so you could read this last chapter, awesome! Because, I personally feel is this chapter is the most important. Either way, I hope you learn something. I hope that this book inspired you. I hope that this book challenged you. I hope that this book made you laugh. I hope that this book made you question things. I hope that this book made you angry. I hope that you experienced a lot of different emotions because I was being real and honest.

My parents are the most amazing parents ever! They are just so supportive and they show me unconditional love. They smack when I need to be smacked, and they hug me when I needed to be hugged. They've been very influential to me regarding the way I see things, the way that I understand individuals, and in the way that I accept people into my heart and mind. I think that my grandmother has also been a very influential person in my life when it comes to pursuing education. One thing that my parents always told me to do, and some people will think this is weird but I still do it today, was to keep a pen and paper next to my bed. I don't know why, but I get my best ideas when I'm asleep. My mind just continues to run and I don't want to forget anything. Keeping the pen and paper next to my bed allows me to wake up in the middle of the night and jot down all those great things. I literally wake up some mornings and there's already a great idea written down. I don't know how it got there; not sure where it came from and I certainly don't know what the heck I was thinking about that night, but I wake up with a phenomenal idea! I was that person, who woke in the morning, turned on the TV and saw those infomercials for some crazy, new invention. I would think "Oh my gosh! I totally should have thought about that!" or "Oh my goodness! I could've come up with that! Now that person is making a million dollars!" How many of you have ever thought like that? That is definitely me. I want to tell you, if you have an idea, a great invention, or you can feel that something is missing in the marketplace, it's up to you to do it. I know a lot of you probably have things that you're always saying you want to do. What I want you to do is come up with three things that you want to do in the next thirty days and then do it! Who's stopping you from doing these things? There are so many objectives we can accomplish, if we just make short-term goals. Thirty days people! That's accomplishing a dream every ten days! What do you want to do? What do you want to create? What's stopping you from pursuing your dreams? This was one of the things that my parents instilled in me for which I will be forever grateful.

I was even making inventions when I was a kid. I remember the summer of 1999. I was ten yearsold, and it was a really hot summer in Philadelphia. This was the summer that three Philadelphia Eagles players collapsed during practice due to heat exhaustion. As a ten yearold kid, I remember that I decided I was going to make this special helmet. This helmet had a special dot on the back that would allow the coach and player personnel to know when a player needed to be taken out due to overheating. Guess what? My parents didn't shut down the idea. They said, "Justin, this is a really great idea; you need to do something with this!" At ten years old, my parents took me to a patent lawyer and I got my idea notarized and copyrighted. I couldn't get my foot into the NFL because it's such a large organization, but that didn't matter. It was the fact that my parents supported me. Whether the idea was dumb or not, it didn't matter. Whether I could do it or not, that wasn't the point either. The point is, my parents supported me. They taught me that you can't just sit on ideas. You need to move them forward; you need to act on them. I know that you all have ideas as well. I would like to tell you that if you haven't done it yet or if you haven't thought about it yet, take the time to think, take the time write, and take your ideas out and make them a reality. Why are you sitting on them? These things can't help you if you're not

163

working on them. Before you read any more of this chapter, I want you to know, this whole book will not help youat all until you're ready to work on yourself.

Throughout this book, we talked about stereotypes, prejudices, perception, women's issues, multicultural awareness, and diversity. We talked about *This or That* and all those other activities and concepts. You probably learned a lot of things that will help you, but until you work on yourself these concepts won't get you anywhere. That's what this chapter is really about – taking the time to work and build on ourselves. None of us are perfect; we're all works in progress. We all have issues and things we need to work on. It's about finding out who you are. If you have found yourself, that's great! If you haven't, I hope that this chapter really encourages you to do so. I like to say, "If you can dream it, you can do it!" A lot of you are sitting on ideas that could change how our world operates. We need to continue to encourage our students to go into the math and sciences. We're only one person or one degree away from the cure to cancer. Why aren't we encouraging more kids to get into the math and sciences? Why aren't we encouraging their creativity and innovation? We represent America, one of the greatest nations on earth, yet we've fallen behind in education and can't keep up. We need to be plucking from everybody; children, teenagers, the elderly, men, women, rich, or poor; everybody has something. If you're dreaming it, you can certainly do it!

I want to let you know that I'm not perfect. I'm not a perfect man – I'm far from it. I have a lot of things that I need to work on. And, I'm not always right. Never in this book did I say that my way is the right way and your way is wrong. There are probably a lot of things in this book that you disagree with and that's great! Why? Because I'm still a young guy and I haven't been around that long. Yes, I've been challenged, stretched,and developed.I've also been told that I was wrong and that I need to look at things in a different way. Throughout my time, I've given my opinions and I've taken heed to the opinions of others. You have to do that as well. If you're not being challenged on a daily basis, you're wasting your time. If you're not being stretched to

164

capacity, you're wasting your time. If you haven't allowed yourself to develop, you're wasting time. We have got to continue to have these concepts and hold them close.

As I said before, I think that life has three best teachers. They don't represent someone who has been in a classroom and they're not a parent, friend, or even a mentor. I think the three greatest teachers in life are heartbreaks, empty pockets, and failures. Unfortunately, I have been the recipient of all three of these things! Let's look at heartbreak – I've had heartbreak, as I'm sure you have as well. Heartbreak is painful, it challenges your morals and values, and it can even make you wonder why you continue. There are people in this world who just don't know how to function alongside another. Like my dad always says, "Hurt people, hurt people." And, people can only meet you where they've already met themselves. Heartbreak is terrible. It makes you want to give up and throw in the towel. It makes you feel abandoned or that you're disposable. It's a giant, life-altering experience.

Now let's think about empty pockets – they are rough! I know people who don't have two pennies to rub together and don't know where their next meal is coming from. They don't know where they're going to be able to find accessible water to wash up or clean their clothes. They don't know where they will find shelter so that they don't freeze in the winter. Empty pockets can really teach you some harsh lessons. I hear kids complaining during the holiday season about not getting the latest iPad. Yet, and yes I'm bringing it up again and will continue to until something is done about it, the citizens of Flint, MI still don't have clean water! Where are our priorities as a country? It's just unacceptable!

Failure is our last teacher. I have failed at a lot of things and it hurts! You feel defeated, you feel discouraged, and ultimately, you question why you tried in the first place. Failure is the best teacher. You're not going to do well at anything if you always know you'll succeed. What would you do if you knew you couldn't fail? What would you try? What would you attempt? Or would you just skate on by? There they are, life's three biggest teachers! Have some or all of these things taught you? What have you gained from the teachings?

I always think this line is pretty funny and I say it to a lot of my students, but it's still pertinent today. This line is "Always be yourself, unless you can be Batman; and if you can be Batman, you should definitely be Batman!" My students laugh and it's funny, but now that I'm thinking more about it, Batman has a lot of significance. You'll see a little bit of my nerdy side coming out with this one! Batman is a representation of what happens when justice isn't served. Batman's parents were killed when he was a kid and the murderer got away. Bruce Wayne had to figure out what he was going to do. The justice system didn't serve him, so he was left with vengeance. He wanted justice and he got it on his own. It's the same thing that's happening in this country to our individuals of color. When justice isn't served, people have to find a means of carrying it out in their own way. It doesn't mean that they should riot, but even riots can be subjective. When there's an injustice affecting the Black community, some people look at Black people who are destroying property and they see it as rioting. But when a sports team wins a championship game and people go out and destroy stuff, why is that not called a riot? We need to pay attention to what's really going on with everyone in this country.

In the same sense, immigration is viewed this way. I think it's so funny, not funny ha-ha, but an ironic funny, that we close our boarders for refugees and immigrants. Yet, that is exactly how this country was started. What we're really saying is that it's okay for people from this country to come here, but it's not okay for people to come here from *that* country. It seems pretty clear how we make the distinction of who is an acceptable immigrant and who is not. This is based off the color of their skin or the God they pray to. How are we deciding these factors? Why is not based on the morality of helping someone in need? Why is it not about bringing new ideas and perspectives into our rich and vibrant communities? I just can't help but think that the answer to protecting the enviornment is in the mind of one of these refugees. But no one was willing to help them survive.

166

Their life was not valued because they were the wrong type of immigrant or refugee.

We need to keep in mind that there are dreamers and there are doers. You don't want to be a dreamer. You're probably thinking that my last statement completely contradicts everything I've shared with you in this book. No, it doesn't – there are differences between dreamers and doers. Dreaming is free, but the hustle is sold separately. What I mean by that is you must be a person of action. There's that one thing on your bucket list that you've always wanted to do. You shouldn't even have a bucket list; there should be nothing in your bucket! Why? Because you should be completing these things every day! You should be moving forward to complete your goals. Who wants to wait until they're fifty years old to start their goals? Who waits until they're on their deathbed before doing something they've always wanted to do? If you've always wanted to do it, do it today! People say, "Why put off today what you can do tomorrow?" I say, "NO! Why put off tomorrow, what you can do today?" Why not get these things done? Being a dreamer is cool – having dreams is great. But being able to have those dreams and make them come true by action is even better!

They put erasers on pencils because everyone makes mistakes, and if you think you're a pen, you're in for world of trouble! We've got people breaking up relationships. We have people being kicked out of church. We constantly see war, crime, and violence on TV. There are a lot of things in this world that can take your joy and happiness away. Wherever you can find little pieces of happiness, take it. Some people find happiness at a Starbucks, some in funny cat videos on YouTube, and some people find through friends and family. There are some people who get their joy from their kids, some people get their joy by going on vacation, and some from reading a good book. Find those things that make you feel happy! Personal wellness is so important people! When you find something that makes you happy and brings you joy, hold on to it. Find other people who enjoy those things and form relationships around that joy.

167

I think that people's beliefs are based upon the realities that they see. If your reality is that everything in America is fine, you're probably going to be greatly disturbed when someone says America is racist, unjust, sexist, or homophobic. You're not going to see or feel those things if they don't directly impact you. Since beliefs are based on only the things individuals see, what I would encourage people to do is wipe the scalesaway from their eyes. Break down the sanctuary of their own thinking in order to see things for what they really are. I'm not saying that you can't think your opinion is right. What I'm saying is, before you make an opinion about something, see both sides. Before you're committed to your opinion, also recognize that other opinions exist and be able to look at things from a different perspective.

Growth is powerful people! Growth creates change, it creates development, and ultimately growth creates personality differences. Growth can be painful and uncomfortable but, we all certainly love the benefits of it. Think about when you were a child and you couldn't reach things that were on the top shelf, you couldn't drive a car, buy a house, or get into the bar. We couldn't wait and we were so happy to finally grow up. So happy, that once we grew up, the first thing we wanted to do was become kids again. Why? Growth is seen as something that is so positive and great. But, I think that growing is actually more rewarding, satisfying, and nurturing than actual growth itself. Once you actually grow, you're there! That's present tense – you already grew and can't go back. The growing process is the part where you learn the lessons. It's the part where you find out more about yourself. It's the part where you are actually making your own set of values. Not the values that your family gave you, the ones you learned in school, or the ones based on your friends. You get to set your own values that can create change in your life and make you who you are.

Think about the things you needed in a person while you were growing up. Someone to mentor you, support and encourage you, someone to tell you everything's going to be alright. Someone who had your back no matter what, and someone who showed up to all of your concerts or sporting events. That person who sent you small notes or a card to cheer you up, the person who would just check up on you for no particular reason, or the person who sent you a text message just to make sure you were operating. Don't forget the person who cooked you a good meal just so you had some food in your belly. Or, the person that said good morning to you because they really hoped that you had a good morning. Be the person that you needed growing up! Be the person you need now. You may only be one person in the world, but you also may be the world to one person. I hate when people say, "I don't need anybody. I'm good on my own." No one can do it all by themselves! We all need people. People say these things because they are hurt or bitter because of something that happened to them. They feel like humanity has failed them. They think that no one can truly be there for them because no has been there for them before. I mean to tell you that everybody needs somebody! We can't do it alone. Be that person you needed when you were growing up or in need.

There are times in my life that I had to be more with less. I've had pains. I've had people hurt me. I've had a door shut right in my face. I've had people laugh at me. I've had people talk about me behind my back. I've had friends completely turn on me. I've had people go out of their way to take me down. I've had people throw my name in the dirt. I've made plans for my life that fell through. When you can't do anything else and you've done all you can, that's how you know your own strength. Sometimes people just have to do more with less. There are a lot of people out there dealing with depression. I'm telling you, don't give up. If you know someone who has depression, get him or her help or be the help that they need; don't give up. We all know people out there who are hurting, who are in pain, who are thinking about taking their lives – you need to be the person those people need. Don't give up. If you're one of those people who are thinking about a job change because you don't think that you're making an impact, don't give up. If you feel that every single thing that you're doing is not effective and not creating change, don't give up. Sometimes you've got to be more with

169

less. Sometimes you've got to fail to succeed. I've shared that failure has been my best teacher because you don't know what you can overcome without failing. I just think that there are more important things to fight for and there are more important things to consider. Failure teaches you those valuable things.

There are more important things that we need to be talking about here in America. Are we swiping the card or inserting the chip? Nobody has come up with a debate or come up with a complete conclusion on this topic. We need to define those things because it's frustrating! That's when failure comes up and it's frustrating. We're not finding a complete and concrete conclusion on things. It's really hard when you fail because it feels like you haven't completed what you set out to do. Failure is really a life-changing component to how we all live and grow. You can't tell me that the sky's the limit when I've seen footprints on the moon. In student affairs we talk a lot about the glass ceiling. I'm here to tell you, we need to break that glass ceiling – let's take a hammer to it! You're only going to be as great as you allow yourself to be. I know that there are systematic frameworks that keep us from reaching certain objectives. I know that there's a wage gap and inequality in a lot of things. I know that the system is designed so that some people always succeed. Despite those things that hold us back, we need to continue to move forward, we need to push through. We need to challenge the status quo. We need to break down walls. I'm tired of using those things as crutches – we can't and we shouldn't. The sky is not the limit for me. You can shoot for the moon, and even if you miss, you're still shining with the stars. We need to continue to do those things.

In life not everybody is going to like you. Let me repeat that, not everybody's going to like you. Suck it up, deal with it! Stop thinking that life was made so everybody can be like you, so you can be popular, so everybody is going to be on board with what you do. You'll end up really disappointed when you go through life thinking people have the same heart as you. As a Christian, I remind myself that not everyone even liked Jesus. So how do you expect everyone to like you? Stop being a fake! Stop trying to be something that you're not so that people can like you! Stop trying to suck up to people so that they accept you! It's just not going to be like that. You can probably list five people right now who hate your guts, and they probably don't even have a reason to hate you. That's what haters do! They find some reason, something about you, and then they hate! But I love my haters because that means there's something so special about me and such a light inside methat I didn't even know that I had. And that made the hater go out of their way to hate me! That shows me that people are paying attention and it shows me that I'm making a difference.

Don't give up on people. You can't. There are people out there that need you. You can probably think of a few people right now who are dependent upon you. It's very easy to give up on people. Giving up is the easy thing to do. The hard thing is to work with people. I'm sure a lot of you are in relationships and even married. Don't give up on people! Some days as a partner, you can't be 100%, sometimes you can only give 60%. You'll need your partner to pick up the slack. That's why we can't give up on people. If you get married, you may take a vow that says for better or for worse. For better or for worse, they're not just words; it has to mean something. If you are getting married just to get married; don't do it! Do it because you really want to be with that person for the rest of your life, do it because that person makes you complete. Do it because you can't live without that person and want to make a commitment to that person. But above all, please make sure that it's a true commitment and not something that you feel in the moment. Feelings change and that's why you need to base it on what you know, not just what you feel. If I punched you in the arm right now, it would probably hurt, but eventually the hurt would go away. That hurt and pain you felt is just a feeling, and it didn't last forever. If you know, in your head, that a punch is always going to hurt, that's not going to change. But feelings can change. If you're truly taking vows and promising to be someone, then you have to be willing to be that same person if the feelings change some over time.

171

I think that people will be happy once they find the courage to let go of what they can't control. As a complete, 100% control freak, I'm here to tell you that. I don't like when the power is taken away from me. I was once told that if you ever want to make God laugh, tell him your plans. Sometimes I feel like I'm a one-man comedy show for God. He's sitting up there laughing at me and probably has some things on repeat! If this show were on DVD, God would buy the Blu-ray special edition with the deleted scenes and blooper reel. I tell God all the time that these are my plans. I come up with all these plans and ideas and I make a timeline on paper. But life doesn't work like that and neither do people. You're literally a couple seconds away from your life changing. Someone could die, you could go bankrupt, you could get sued, or you could be in a car accident. Anything could happen at any time, just in the blink an eye. You can't control every single thing in your life. You can have a plan but your plans aren't always going to happen the way you want them to. Do you get mad at God because he didn't give you what you wanted when you wanted it? Are you mad at God because He shut the door in your face or because your plans didn't go the way you wanted them to? Are you just going to give up and throw in the towel because it didn't go your way? You can't do that! You have got to continue to move forward despite the events that take place. And, when you finally decide to let go, you truly have to do it. Believe me, letting go takes courage, you can't just "let go." It's not as easy as that. Is anyone else singing "Let It Go" from the movie *Frozen* right now, or is it just me? Everyone was so obsessed with that song! But anyway, it takes courage, pride, and humility to let go. Some things that we don't want to let go aren't good for us but we have to follow through to move forward.

Some days you have to make your own sunshine. I know there's a lot of people who come to me, and probably come to you as well, for encouragement. But, sometimes people need to encourage themselves. Sometimes you have to be your own cheerleader. I'm telling you that I've gone through things in my life where I literally had to wake up in the morning, look myself in the mirror and say, "Today is going to be a good day!" Good days are not dependent on other people, you determine them. If you had $3,000 and somebody stole $5 of it, are you going to shred the other $2,995? No! You're going to keep that money. So, if you have 1,440 minutes in a day, are you going to allow somebody who messed up five minutes destroy the remaining 1,435 minutes? It's the same concept. We can't allow people to do that. We have got to be able to make our own sunshine, encourage ourselves, and have our own self-esteem. That's why it's called *self*-esteem. While it's great to rely on people to help boost us up, what are you doing to boost yourself? What are the things you're doing to encourage yourself? How are you making the best out of your day? Creating your own sunshine is extremely important.

I want to know why people are waiting for permission to be great. Every single one of us is made from a different cloth − different backgrounds, experiences, situations, lessons that were taught to us, and ways of living. Why are you waiting for permission to be great? You want to be great, but maybe you haven't gotten there yet. What are you waiting for? Get off your butt, go do something you haven't tried before, go learn something, go eat food you've never tried, or travel to a different country. Why are you waiting for permission? Go out there and make something of yourself. I want to hear about you. Right now, you probably never met me but if you did, you would be thinking, "I knew Justin was going to write a book one day." but you weren't waiting for me to do it. I wanted to do it, I went out there and I completed it. The time for *what ifs* is over. Get it done.

In life there are only a few people care, the rest are just curious. Your value does not decrease based on someone's inability to see your worth. You've got to be able to operate with who's in your life for a season, and with who's supposed to be in your life forever. You can't be upset because in your story of life, some people choose to walk out. Just like on TV, some characters get written off, it just happens. Obviously you're going to be sad about it but it just means that their part of the

173

story is over. You have to carry on to the next episode. There are going to be some people coming into you're your life and maybe it's only for one season – a guest appearance. Unfortunately, it's like that. Sometimes their character is only on the show for a few episodes and then they leave for whatever reason. You can't make other people's problems your problem. I'm sure a lot of you are thinking, "Why didn't that person stay...they were supposed to be my friend? Or, if you're thinking about a relationship, "Why did that person leave me? What did I do wrong?" Again, you can't make other people's issues your issues. People do things all the time for whatever reason they want, sometimes, just because they want to. It has nothing to do with you. You could have treated them like a queen or a king and they still left, so why are you sitting here worrying about people who want nothing to do with you. There are plenty of other people who care about you and want what is the best for you. Those are the people you need to pay attention to. Those people are your support system and that's where your central focus needs to be.

I think people need to focus on who they are – their business and their actions. I don't want to talk, I want to act. I don't want to say, I want to show. I don't want to promise, I want to prove. Listen, people with integrity are very predictable. As Justin LaKyle Brown, I know that I'm a man of routine too. If you know me, you probably know my routine. You know what time I'm getting up, when I'm eating lunch, whether it's TV time or work out time, and you know what time I'm going to bed. I'm tired of just being a person who says stuff. I want to be somebody who people recognize, if I said I'll do something then I can and will. I want to be somebody that will take care of something if I said I would take care of it – a man of my word. Don't you want to have a reputation of being a person that's about business and action, not just talk? Those are the legacies you leave behind. Those are the things that you teach your kids and your grandkids. Those are the examples to show other people.

Do you know that sometimes the only Bible that some people will read is your life? I don't have to go out and say, "I'm a Christian! I'm a Christian! Be a Christian!" No, I don't have to do that. People know I'm a Christian based on how I speak, how I treat others, and how I live my life. Don't you think that's more of a turning point for people than trying to force them to change just because I want them to? That's a better witness than forcing the Bible down someone's throat. Sometimes it's not even about religion because they're just good people that are out there. Good people do exist; not everybody in this world is out to get you or hurt you. One of the best things that my friend Terrece told me was, "Always keep your guard up." In any situation, anything can go awry, anything can go sideways. It's great that you want to help people. You could probably think to yourself right now, who's the nicest person in your life? They probably get taken advantage of because everyone likes them and they can't say no to anyone – or is this person you? They're the person that probably gets hurt the most. How many of you wear your heart on your sleeve? It happens. It makes us very susceptible to get hurt.

My friend Terrece told me to always keep my guard up, why? Because as my friend, he wanted to protect me, himself, and others around him. Just because you have your guard up, doesn't mean you can't put your guard down. What he did tell me was, you don't put up a wall. If you put up a wall, it can help you, or it could hurt you. Walls were made to keep things out. A wall doesn't let anything in or out, kind of like a double-edged sword. Are you letting people in? Are you truly opening up to new relationships and trying new things? Or, do you have a wall put up and you're living the same bitter life you do every day? If you're stuck on something that you've been stuck on for five years, you've got to let it go. If there are people you had issues with, go reconcile and put the pieces of the puzzle back together. Stop waiting for somebody to call you and apologize. Sometimes you have to take the loss and move on. Sometimes we have to accept the apologies that were never given to us. And, sometimes we got to be able to move forward without other people's blessing or forgiveness. Sometimes you have to make peace and apologize, even if it's small, and even if you don't think you

175

were completely in the wrong. Imagine if everybody took responsibility for things, even some things they didn't do, how much better of a world this would be? If everybody said, "I know that this was primarily your fault, but regardless, I still hold some responsibility in this too because maybe I could've handled it differently." Imagine what the world would be like if everybody took responsibility for the parts they play. Wouldn't we work together so much more smoothly? In any situation, everybody should take part of the blame. No one person is ever 100% responsible.

Sometimes, people suck. I'd be lying if I told you that my entire life was full of individuals who supported me and wanted the best for me. While I have my strong supporters, I also was faced with many, many people who wanted to see me fail and enjoyed putting me down. These people were in all parts of my life – colleagues, friends, church folk, past relationships – people who just did not want me to be successful. My advice for you on this is that you have to push forward regardless. Identify the fakes and watch out for the traps. Not everyone with a friendly smile on their face is actually a friend. Life isn't about the amount of friends you have, it's about the influence and memories your true friends had on you.

I know that a lot of you don't believe in God or Jesus and that's fine. I'm not here to tell you that you should. I think a lot of Christians try to force their beliefs and people don't want to hear that, and I understand. We can't get people to understand Christ when we're also saying and doing the same thing everyone else is doing. So, I'm not going to tell you to believe in Christ. Do I wish that you could? Yeah, but I don't wish you could because that's what I believe. I'm not pushing my beliefs on you. What I do want you to think is, you don't have to believe in God, but believe in something. Whether you believe in Allah, or practice Buddhism, Judaism, Scientology, or even if you believe in Goku, it doesn't matter. I just need you to believe in something. If you don't believe in any of those beings, at least believe in yourself. There are people that go around having no beliefs. Where do you base your understanding of life? How do

176

you make connections work? Where do you get your values? You've got to believe in something. Does somebody believe in you? We have to believe in people too. Like I said previously, a lot of the time we give up on people. Do you really, in your heart, believe that people can change? Or are people always going to be the way they are? Everyone deserves a fair chance. I can only imagine where I would be if someone hadn't given me a chance or a shot. We have to be able to give people their shot too. Once they take it, it's on them. But, we should know that people want to do better for themselves. Some people want to be better, and for the people who don't, let them do what they do.

You can't be a leader if you're not ready to take L or the losses. If you don't want to take an L, don't be a leader because there are a lot of times that I had to receive one, even though it wasn't on me. But it was my responsibility as the leader. There were times as the leader I had to apologize even though I didn't do anything wrong. The times that I had to take responsibilities for things that didn't take place or didn't happen even though they weren't necessarily my fault. Leadership requires you to do more. And, leading is not always from the front. I know a lot of great leaders that lead from the back. We've got to be able to shut that mentality of thinking down. Leaders come in a variety of shapes, colors, sizes, ethnicities, and different belief systems. Not every leader is an extrovert. Not every person who does great presentations is an extrovert. Not all introverts hate hanging out with people. We have to get out of the mindset that all leaders are a certain way. Anybody can be a leader, but it takes somebody with strength, humility, pride, and excellence to fill that role. Let life surprise you – sometimes you just have to go for it. Do you know how many times in life things didn't go the way I wanted them to that and they actually ended up working out better? We have to be able to let life be flexible. Things can't just go according to your plan. If you're not flexible, you're going to bend and you're going to break. We all know what it's like to break – to want to give up, to not be motivated, and to just want throw in the towel. Is that you right now? Let life surprise you. Go outside and bask in the sun, go

177

meet somebody you've never met, go eat a food you've never tried, watch a movie you normally wouldn't, just try something new. When was the last time you called that one friend you haven't talked to in a while? Meet up with them and catch up on life or go read a book. Look at old pictures on Facebook and reminisce about what you did in college. Are you the same person? Have you really grown? These are things that life can surprise us with. Give people chances, they might just surprise you as well.

The walls that you build for yourself only confine you. How many walls are you building? How thick are you making them? If you had to take your walls down right now, could you? Man, these walls can be rough, they don't let anyone in and they sure don't let us out! Walls are dangerous because they keep you separated from things that can help you. If you have a wall up, how can you go out and get the stuff that you're going to need in order to grow? How are you going to go out there and meet new people and have new experiences? Walls, while they're great for protection, they're horrible for growth. They confine you and limit your possibilities. So yes, even as the author of this book on diversity, I have walls too. When I was writing this book, walls of doubt confined me. Will my book be good? Will people read it? Am I going to be criticized? Are people going to just look at this book and say, "Man, he just went off...none of these things are even related. It was all over the place. I can't follow what he's saying." But for me, I can't be confined by those walls of skepticism or by the walls of fear. So, I decided to put a door on this wall. That way, the wall is still up, but I had the ability to go in and out. I can take constructive criticism. I can take that not everybody is going to like the text. But I will not allow myself to be confined by these walls. This means that there are times when I'm going to need to come out and sometimes I'm going to be a little vulnerable, and that's okay. Being vulnerable, means you're human. Being vulnerable, means your imperfect. Not all walls are immune to penetration, sometimes people get in and that's okay too. Maybe they are there for reason.

If you haven't failed at anything, you haven't tried hard

enough. Don't be afraid to ask for help. If you need counseling, take it. It's okay to say you're not okay! People want to be strong and not show signs of weakness. But, you can't be strong everyday of your life. There's going to come a time when you will need help and support. No one is a one-person show. Sometimes you have to take the plunge and start caring about something with all your heart and energy. You have to know that you can't fully and truly care about it if you are holding yourself back. This fear will prevent you from succeeding.

I don't think you always make the right choice. I think you make a choice and then you make it right. A lot of times we choose things, thinking they're the best for us, only to find out that they're not. When that happens to most people, they kind of just pout and say, "Well, I didn't want that to happen and now that it happened, I guess I just have to deal with it." No! Make the best out of your situation. You need to align yourself with people who fit your destiny not your history. If you go on vacation and it's raining, who cares?! Some people don't get to go on vacation! Make the best out of that situation; go dance in the rain, go to a movie, or just take a nap. When life gives you lemons, don't just make the lemonade, make a lemon pie too! Do you know how many situations didn't work out for me? What did I do? I made the best out of it and it ended up being better than planned. Why? Because I took the initiative. Where's the initiative people? Where's the drive? Where's the pizzazz? Where's the creativity? We have to get back to those things. Those are the things that make life fun for us – the things that make life enjoyable and even sometimes, those are the things that make life worth living.

Normal is a fantasy. What is normal to a wolf is chaos to a sheep. We have to break these self-prescribed norms. We need to be able to do things that are different. I can't live in normal. I need to do something new. I have to go out. I have to challenge my own thinking. I've got to go against what I originally thought I would do. I have to keep my mind open knowing that there are other possibilities out there. And that is hard for me, because as Justin, I like things my way. I know some of you who know me

179

personally are probably thinking, "Yup, he sure does!" I like things my way and I can be impatient, both of those are very true. They don't make me a bad person; they just make me a human. Who wants to be normal anyway? Who wants to live a normal life? Who wants to live a boring, careful life? Sometimes you've got to be carefree. Sometimes you've got to break down the existence of your old thinking. Just get out there!

We need to make a legacy, and you can only make a legacy once there's revolution. Revolution can only be created once people are inspired. Are you inspired? Did the book inspire you? Were there things in it that you could take and learn from? I truly hope so. I spent a lot of time creating this book – it is probably about 10 years in the making. In my Diversity Awareness Programs, no one learns more than I do. That happens because I'm more than a participant. I'm more than a presenter. I'm more than a facilitator. I'm someone who's conducting a focus group. So, the almost 400 schools I visited were a giant focus group; giant surveys or assessment tools that helped me figure out what is going on in people's lives. How can I get a grasp of it? What do I need to do as a professional to help meet people's needs where they are at;not just one person, but everybody. It's always a beautiful day to change lives and I always want to do that. Do you want to change lives? Are you making an impact? I hope so. My goal with this book was to be able to change your life. Have I been able to do that? I just know that there are a lot of great people out there. More importantly, there are a lot of great people out there who don't know that they're great...yet.

Be the person who can be great for somebody else. Continue to strive, kick down doors, and be awesome. I always tell my students, "Don't be dope, live dopely." This means be the best version of you. In life, you should only be competing with yourself. Make yourself a better version of you. Take time to get to know you. Take time to work on yourself. Take time to be the best person you can be. As Justin LaKyle Brown, I'm signing off. I'll be here whenever you need me; all you have to do is read the last chapter of this book. I'm here – these are my words. This is where my heart is and like I said, when you're looking for me, you'll find me in the crowd of life changers. You'll find me in the crowd of those who are servant leaders. You'll find me in the place that's trying to make a difference in people's lives. If this book was helpful to you, I hope that you'll pass it on to someone else that needs it too. Think about someone else who may need some words of encouragement. Consider someone else who is trying to learn, because that's what it's all about. When you know better you do better.

Peace.

Justin L. Brown

About the Author

Justin L. Brown is a renowned presenter and critically acclaimed speaker who has devoted his life to educating campuses, businesses, and society about cultural awareness. Justin helps to build the respect of others, communication, authentic relationships, and how to have a closer connection to God. After being fed up with the world and its continuing decline of respect, morals, and values, Justin was determined to make a difference. Justin's passion is for working with students developed while pursuing a bachelor's degree in public relations from Slippery Rock University. During his undergraduate tenure, Justin was actively involved on campus through working and collaborating with various offices and departments. It was during this time that Justin created the Diversity Awareness Program (D.A.P.), a program dedicated to raising awareness and educating college campuses about the importance of diversity and embracing all cultures and backgrounds. Justin then continued nurturing D.A.P. through his graduate studies at the Indiana University of Pennsylvania, while working towards earning his master's degree in Student Affairs in Higher Education. D.A.P. has successfully grown in popularity, having visited over 400 colleges and universitiesand established over 20 chapterswithin those institutions. For a while, parents, friends, and professors had been asking Justin to put his ideas and concepts into a book that everyone could use and learn from. This book is the product of that demand.

About Diversity Awareness Program

The purpose of D.A.P. is to encourage diversity and cultural unity in all areas of life among students, faculty, and staff on a university campus. This will be accomplished through energetic and vigorous engagements and dynamic discussions on issues and ideas. D.A.P. will serve as a catalyst in encouraging students and community members to search for opportunities to become more culturally aware and conscious.

This organization has educated students around the country by inviting a diverse group of people together to participate in activities that not only help them to know each other in small groups, but also to have discussion topics as a large group.

The energy and commitment of the collective whole of its membership is amazingly strong. It has approximately over 50,000 members meeting weekly; voluntarily coming together to discuss, role play, and challenge each other on social issues, ideas, personal relationships, stereotypes, cultural identities, and so much more.

If you would like to donate to the Diversity Awareness Program Scholarship Fund, please contact Justin directly.

If interested in the program, please view our website.

http://diversityawareness.wix.com/program

To schedule Justin for a keynote speech, assembly, convocation, seminar, workshop, educational convention or training session, please contact:

Justin L. Brown
40 Lauren Lane
Coatesville Pa, 19320

Justin will customize and format any program to fit the needs
and expectations of the organization or audience.

Contact Justin directly: **Email:** justinbrown331@gmail.com